Childless
No More

SHARON AIKMAN

Childless

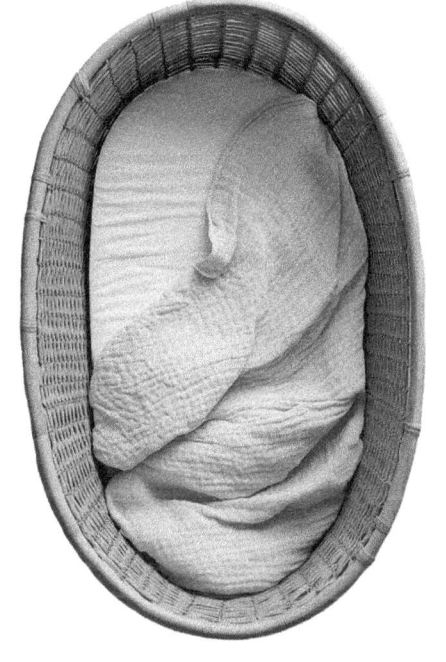

No More

SOMETIMES GOD ANSWERS PRAYERS BY CHANGING THEM

Childless No More

© 2024 by Sharon Aikman

Published by Truth Book Company, LLC
Anderson, IN

All rights reserved. No part of this publication may be reproduced, stored in a retrieval system or transmitted in any form by any means, electronic, mechanical, photocopy, recording, or otherwise, without the prior permission of the publisher, or author, except as provided by USA copyright law.

ISBN 979-8-9895526-9-6, *paperback*

Cover Design & Typesetting: Truth Book Company, LLC

Scripture quotations from The Authorized (King James) Version unless otherwise noted. Rights in the Authorized Version in the United Kingdom are vested in the Crown. Reproduced by permission of the Crown's patentee, Cambridge University Press. Added emphasis has been noted.

We hope you enjoy this book from Truth Book Company. Our goal is to provide high-quality, Bible-based books, curriculum, and resources to equip you to stand for truth.

You can contact Sharon Aikman at **sharon.aikman@gmail.com**.

For more information on our other books and resources, special discounts, bulk purchases, or hosting a live event, please visit **www.truthbook.co**.

To my husband Chuck and our children Noah, Lexi, Kayla, Lilly, Nathan, Jazzy, Nevaeh, Christopher, Ian, and Mia—this is for you. May you feel the love I have for each of you and never forget you were hand-picked by God to answer my prayers.

Table of Contents

Chapter 1	The Dream	3
Chapter 2	The Journey	9
Chapter 3	A Mother's Day Promise	43
Chapter 4	The Death of a Promise	67
Chapter 5	The Promise Fulfilled	73
Chapter 6	New Beginnings	85
Chapter 7	The Vision Becomes a Reality	97
Chapter 8	The Arrival of Nathan	107
Chapter 9	Conversations with the Lord	111

CHAPTER 1

The Dream

As far back as I can remember, I pretended to be a mother. As a child, I was always playing house. Even before I could pretend and make up games, I played the role of "little Mother." My mother was only eighteen when I was born, and she relied very heavily on me. She used to tell me I was destined to be a mother. Because I was born on Mother's Day, I was sure she was correct.

When I was twenty-two months old, my baby brother was born. Mom told many stories about how I anticipated having a baby of my own during her delivery. Mom would say that I was still in diapers when he was born, but by the time I was twenty-four months old, I was completely potty trained because "mommies don't wear diapers." For me, the path to motherhood was set at the birth of my baby brother, Ricky Dale.

From my earliest memories, I can recall our days at home on the Anderson farm. Farm life created many opportunities for nurture and motherhood.

One spring, when I was about four years old, we had a lamb named Oscar whose mother had rejected him at birth. My mother and father diapered the new lamb and brought him into the house to bottle-feed him until he was mature enough to be out in the barnyard with the other animals. I could not wait to help with his feedings and diapering! I remember kissing him good night and saying my prayers with him before tucking him into the hamper to sleep each night. Oscar was a challenging little one because he romped and rough-housed. Eventually, he got into trouble with the family dog, Frosty, because Oscar had head-butted little Ricky. Ricky was toddling around and not able to defend himself against the rambunctious lamb. That was the day our father decided it was time for Oscar to be outdoors. I was sad that Oscar could no longer sleep in the house, but I was happy to see him in the barnyard playing with the other lambs and growing strong.

Sadly, my parents had a tumultuous relationship and soon divorced. This immediately put me into a leading role in caring for Ricky while Mom was facing her new life as a single mother and dealing with her own pain. Mom was often working, so I spent most of my time entertaining and caring for me and Ricky.

During those years, I recall playing house, directing Ricky in daily chores, teaching him to have manners, and always having lots of play. I cherish those memories.

At age seven, I received a precious gift—my baby sister. The world became wonderful the day she came home.

THE DREAM

I thought to myself, "This precious little bundle to love, dress up, rock, read stories to..." Oh, the fun we were going to have!

I can remember watching my mother's belly grow. She would often tell me how one day I would be pregnant and that I was next in line for twins! My maternal grandfather was a twin, and my mother believed that it was my turn next. I could hardly wait!

To me, I was now mothering two children and loving every moment. My mother was in a new relationship with the man who eventually became my stepfather. Wimpy, as we called him, was in a country western band. Every weekend the band played gigs, and for several years we spent every Friday and Saturday night with a babysitter. I felt responsible for the kids, and I took my responsibility of caring for them very seriously when our mother was not around. Mom would thank me for the good care I took of my siblings, encouraging me to always look out for them.

When I look back over my life, there is not a time I can recall when I was not mothering.

When I was in the second and third grades, my baby sister Deede went to daycare, but Ricky and I stayed home alone before and after school. Once again, I was placed in charge of caring for him. I dressed Ricky, made our breakfast, and put us on the school bus every morning. I wore a house key on a thick yarn string around my neck to allow us into the house after getting off the school bus. You can see the key in my third-grade school photos. Upon arriving home each afternoon, I made sure we followed house rules for safety. We had a snack and checked homework, all the while keeping Ricky entertained and safe. Once, I remember trying to make pancakes and had the gas burner on too high. The grease caught fire, but thank God my oldest stepbrother was home and ran into the kitchen and stopped me just as I was about to pour water on a grease fire! He threw flour on it and gruffly educated me on the types of fires and appropriate ways to extinguish each one. I am thankful for that lesson, and I remember it vividly to this day.

When my stepfather's first wife died, their four older children came to live in our home. This was, of course, a huge change for all of us, and it was full of challenges. In many ways, we were all finding our new roles in the family. I continued to act as the little mother and became my mother's right-hand help. I was no longer the eldest of the children living in the house. Having older girls in the house telling me what to do was a big adjustment to my life.

By the age of ten, my mother had a home daycare, so I was helping care for many children. We played house every day—of course, I played the mother.

I would corral kids to get them ready for the school bus, watching over them while we waited, making sure no one got too close to the road or forgot their lunch sacks.

Eventually, Mom went back to work, closed the daycare, and again left me in charge of the before-and-after-school children and all that went along with it.

By the age of twelve, I was making dinner most nights, helping plan meals, grocery shopping, and constantly reading magazine recipes to try new things.

Mom was not a fan of being in the kitchen. She would say, "The only reason we have a kitchen was because it came with the house!" Unlike her, I would be happy to live in a kitchen with nothing else but a cot to sleep on.

In the mornings, I would make breakfast for everyone, learning how to make French toast and serving my little family. The Lord was preparing me to have gifts of hospitality and love toward others—two things that would become so important to me later in life.

In my teenage years, my girlfriends and I would dream of our future husbands, our families, our homes, and our cars. I knew that I would marry young, become a nurse (my only other lifelong dream), and have many children. I would have a house, a station wagon, and an old English Sheepdog. Being a mother was not optional to me—it was natural. It was my destiny.

CHAPTER 2

The Journey

By the age of twenty, I was ready to have a baby and become a mother. Unfortunately, I was in an abusive relationship and knew it was not the right environment for my dreams to be realized. Eventually, I was able to escape the abusive partner, but I was also having severe issues with my menstrual cycles. I attributed the long and painful cycles to the stress in my life. Combined, these issues made it very difficult for me to become pregnant.

By the age of twenty-two, I married and began a concerted effort to become pregnant. My husband had a little boy who was a delight to my soul, and I looked forward to every other weekend when his son was with us. It was fulfilling, yet at the same time painful. While I wanted nothing more than to have a child of my own, my family welcomed my stepson into our circle with open arms and showered him with love and attention. That little boy has grown into a wonderful man with a wife and daughter of his own.

By twenty-four, it was clear to me that I was having fertility issues. For five years, I had refrained from using any kind of birth control and still had not become pregnant. I decided that it was time to see a doctor.

During my first appointment, I was told that I was fifty pounds overweight and instructed to lose weight. After that, I would return to the doctor for another check-up. I left the appointment devastated. I could hear a voice in my head telling me that I did not deserve to be pregnant. Although I had tried dieting for many years, I felt as though I were being told that due to my weight, I was unfit to become a mother.

I suffered infertility for another year before seeing a new doctor in our area who was known for his fertility practice. My first appointment began with an office visit and a basal temperature chart. After three months of monitoring these numbers, it was clear that I was not ovulating. By that time, my monthly cycles were no longer monthly. When they did happen, they were lengthy with intense pain, cramps, and other symptoms. We now know that I had Polycystic Ovarian Syndrome (PCOS) as well as Endometriosis, but at the time, neither was commonly diagnosed. I had all the classic symptoms and the many unpleasant experiences that, at times, left me discouraged. While PCOS can be effectively treated today, at that time, I was largely left to deal with the symptoms and manage the pain.

THE JOURNEY

Once it was clear that I was not ovulating, I was prescribed a medication called Clomid. The medicine had difficult side effects but was intended to stimulate fertility. I put a great deal of faith in the drug and believed it would be my path to becoming a mother.

While on this medication, I experienced many unpleasant side effects, including an intense foggy feeling in my head. Strangely enough, if I went into shopping venues or buildings with big overhead lights it was like I was in a dream. I couldn't seem to clear my head. If I stayed in a store for any length of time, my symptoms would worsen, and I would become so ill that I would have to leave. There were times when I had to stop what I was doing, abandon the shopping cart, and walk away just to find some relief. I continued the basal temperature chart with the daily Clomid for six months with no results. Eventually, my doctor took me off the medication and scheduled more testing.

While I was struggling with fertility issues, my baby sister, Deede, was seventeen years old and dating a young man who worked with our mother.

Deede had not been feeling well, so Mother and I took her to the doctor. She was losing weight and sleeping a lot, and we feared she needed to have her appendix removed. While at the doctor's appointment, she was asked if there was any chance she could be pregnant. Of course, we all believed this was impossible, but the doctors insisted on giving her a pregnancy test before any other assessment.

Indeed, she was pregnant. I cannot put into words the emotions I felt in those first moments after hearing Deede was pregnant. I knew it would change her life forever. After all, she was only a senior in high school with plans to attend college. Admittedly, I also struggled with envy upon hearing the news. I could not believe that my baby sister would be a mother before me. It was shocking and painful.

I could not comprehend the news of Deede's pregnancy. How would I move forward to support my sister while at the same time hiding my own pain? The feeling of supporting others in their pregnancies while experiencing the intense pain of infertility was a battle I had not yet fought but one that I would become very familiar with in the years to come.

When you are childless and desperately want to be a mother, you become keenly aware of other pregnant women, babies crying, ultrasound photos, news stories of abused children, and everything related to children and pregnancy. It is a state of mind that compares to nothing else.

Eventually, the time came for Deede's first ultrasound. It was a Tuesday, and I was at work. My mother, sister, and her boyfriend had gone to the first appointment. Following the doctor's visit, the three of them came to where I worked with the ultrasound photo in hand. I remember how excited my mother was, showing anyone who would look what was on the ultrasound. Then I saw the photo, and I could not believe my eyes. There was not one, but two babies in the photo. My sister, who was seventeen and still in high school, was now pregnant with twins.

"MY twins!" I thought to myself.

My head was spinning. My entire life, I had been told that I would have twins. Whenever I imagined my life as an adult, I was always the mother of twins. I didn't know how I would get through the rest of the day, the pregnancy —even my life.

I was also disheartened at my mother's joy. Didn't she realize how this would affect my sister? What about how it would affect me? While trying not to reveal the searing pain in my heart and mind, I was surprised at my mother's response. Was I simply experiencing jealousy? Sadness? I had never felt such raw and painful emotion. Deede was my baby—the absolute love of my life. From the time she was born, Deede was the one I cared for more than anything in the world. Nevertheless, I now faced her with confusion. I wanted to be happy for her, but I could not ignore my own feelings of disappointment. I tried to conceal my emotions from her, but it was a conflict in my heart that was not easy to resolve.

As Deede's pregnancy progressed, she had many complications. She suffered from severe nausea and vomiting, then began having contractions very early on, requiring multiple hospitalizations to stop them so that the twins would survive. Eventually, she was taken by ambulance to Indianapolis so that—should she go into labor—she would be next door to a world-renowned children's hospital to give the babies the best chance of survival. Fortunately, after several days in the hospital, she was discharged on strict bed rest and would remain so until the twins arrived. It was a long pregnancy with multiple frightening moments. The babies arrived one month early, healthy, and absolutely perfect in every way.

During Deede's pregnancy, my fertility testing continued. I had a hysterosalpingogram, which revealed complications in my uterus. My doctor met with me after the procedure and said it was clear I needed intervention to be able to conceive. Surgery was scheduled for April 1990.

☙

Our hospital had purchased a new laser, and I would be the first patient to have the laser used on them surgically. I was excited and scared. I recall going into the surgery knowing this was my answer, and I was going to wake up ready to conceive. I believed all my waiting was about to come to fruition.

I arrived at the hospital at 6 am for the surgery, and my mother and husband were with me, offering much support. Still, I was not nervous at all.

The day before my surgery was Easter Sunday. Prior to that day, I hadn't gone to church in many years, but I decided to attend service that Easter. My precious mother-in-law had been talking to me about salvation and the goodness of God. It was impossible to have a conversation with her of any kind and not hear about her faith and love for God. I knew I needed God in my life, and I had gone to church as a child. I also knew He was real, and I knew He was calling me closer to Him. Around that time, I had purchased a Living Bible and had been reading it.

My brother and sister-in-law visited me the day before Easter, and they invited myself and my husband to join them for church the next morning. I said yes. My husband did not wish to go, but he encouraged me to do so. I got up the next morning, drove to the church, and parked in the back. I got out of my car, and suddenly tears began to flow down my face. What was happening? Why was I such a mess? I walked up the stairs and entered the door to a full church house that was standing room only. An usher brought me a chair, and I sat up against the wall in the back. I could not take my eyes off the painting behind the pulpit. It was a painting of Jesus rescuing a lamb from a thicket. What was that? It spoke to me deeply. I don't recall a single word that was preached, though I vividly recall one song, Gentle Hands, that was sung so beautifully. I needed to find this Jesus they were singing of and let Him into my heart. Something had changed in my soul during that moment. I cried and cried and cried.

ഗ

Easter Sunday afternoon, I asked my husband if he would go to church with me that evening, and again, he said no, but he encouraged me to do so if I wanted. I don't think anything could have stopped me from going back to service that night. At the altar call, I was the first one to come forward. I couldn't wait to kneel and ask the Lord to forgive my sins. I prayed for some time, got up, and left. After service, I was feeling so anxious that I immediately drove to the convenience store down the road to purchase a pack of cigarettes.

At the time, I was smoking more than two packs per day. As I purchased the cigarettes, I turned around, and there was one of the women from the church who had prayed with me at the altar. This precious, godly woman placed her hand on top of mine—my hand that was holding the cigarettes—and began to say how amazing it was to see me in the altar. She told me that the Holy Ghost was all over me! She was sure God had a plan for my life, and she couldn't wait to see what He had in store. All the while, I was deeply embarrassed because this holy woman was touching those horrible cigarettes I had shamefully purchased in my angst. I walked out the door and tossed my cigarettes into the trash can to my left, and I have never touched them again. As of the writing of this book, it has been thirty-four years since I stopped smoking. It was the first miracle in my life!

I had been trying to stop smoking for three years, and I thought I had tried everything. I did not want to smoke during a pregnancy or around a baby. I had even gone through a lengthy hiring process for a high-paying job, but when I went in for the physical to complete the hiring process, I was dismissed. The Doctor conducting the physical told me that at the rate I was going, I would require oxygen before I was thirty and that at twenty-four years old, my body was experiencing pre-emphysema levels of lung failure. I had been smoking since I was twelve years old, and though I tried many times, I could not quit. But that is the power of the Holy Ghost! In a moment, after one service, one sister placing her hand on the cigarettes, I was delivered from an addiction I could not break on my own. God's miraculous power was already at work in my life.

After that Easter Sunday, I was scheduled for an 8 am surgery. Joy filled my soul since I had been touched by the Master himself, awakened with new hope, and had zero desire for a cigarette. On a spiritual level, a change had taken place in me at the altar the evening prior. I didn't understand what was happening, but I wanted more of it.

I found myself humming the tune of *Gentle Hands* while I was being wheeled into the operating room with no fear at all. I was in the hands of the almighty God, and I knew that all would be well.

When I awakened from the surgery, I was wheeled upstairs to my hospital room, where I would recover for a few days. I asked my nurse what time it was because it was dark outside. Was it evening already? "Yes," she said, "it's now 8 pm." I was confused. Had something gone wrong during the surgery? Why had it taken twelve hours? Surely, I should have been awake before then. Still feeling groggy, I inquired about the lateness of the hour again, but the doctor insisted that he would speak with me in the morning about what had transpired during the surgery. Of course, I was concerned. I also realized that there was something on my legs. The nurse explained that I had Teflon leads in my fallopian tubes, and they were now taped to my legs. She told me that it was important that I not pull them out during the night because they were critical to what had transpired during the surgery. I cautiously agreed, and she left.

I recall two comical things about the evening of my surgery. When I arrived at my hospital room post-operatively, my stepfather was in my room. I giggled at his new haircut. For some reason, that struck me as funny, and it hurt to laugh. He said perhaps he needed a new barber for next time and laughed with me. The second thing I noticed was a large, peach-colored, round beach ball appearing in the corner chair of the room. It was my baby sister! It was Deede's very pregnant belly one month prior to the birth of the twins! She was wearing a peach-colored shirt that accentuated the circumference and size of her precious middle.

The next morning, my surgeon and anesthesiologist came in to discuss the events of the surgery. The anesthesiologist instructed me in breathing exercises and encouraged me to continue not smoking. I assured him that God had delivered me, and I was on the path to restoring lung health by never smoking again.

My gynecologist, who had performed the surgery, explained many issues he discovered throughout the

THE JOURNEY

course of the surgery. I had multiple areas of scar tissue called adhesions, and the adhesions had attached to my fallopian tubes and adhered to my bowel in several places, creating complications with other parts of my body. The laser was used to remove multiple areas of the tissue that were creating complications. The next step was to go into the uterus and create openings in the tubes so that my eggs could leave the ovaries to travel down the tubes and become fertilized and implant into the uterine lining. He said that once the openings were created, they (his partner had been called to join him due to the findings once he opened my abdomen) began the very long process of breaking up the many blockages in both tubes.

The surgeon explained that he would use the laser to break up a blockage, only to find a very small clearing followed by another blockage of scar tissue. This was the case in both tubes. On the right fallopian tube, there was a place where even the laser could not break through, requiring an end-to-end anastomosis, a procedure of cutting the tube, removing the blocked section, and then reattaching the tube with sutures. Once both tubes were cleared, it was discovered that my tubes did not have fimbriae on the ends, small fingers that catch the released eggs from the ovaries and sweep them into the tubes to travel to the uterus. Using the laser, fimbria were created. After the work on the uterus and tubes was completed, the ovaries did not appear to have holes in them to release the eggs during ovulation. Tiny holes were made into the ovaries using the new laser technology, procedures that would not have been possible without it.

Finally, Teflon guide wires used for heart catheterization were placed into my uterus and threaded into my tubes. This was to keep them open while they healed, allowing a path for the eggs to travel once released. My surgeon held my hand so gently and said, "Prior to this surgery yesterday, you had no chance of a pregnancy. It was impossible for you to conceive, but now you have *some* chance. Get pregnant quickly." He went on to say that, although it was not clear why, my body was creating scar tissue in large amounts. It would be difficult for me to conceive, and with the odds against me, time was running out.

Thankfully, my surgeon was a man of faith, and he prayed with me that all would work in my favor. In good humor, he said that post-op, the first thing I said was, "Am I pregnant yet?"

After a five-day hospitalization, I was released and headed home with a renewed sense of hope. I could not wait for the birth of my sister's twins, and I was excited to think that my turn at pregnancy was not far away.

Because of the demand on our family's time, I stayed with Deede during the closing months of her pregnancy. If anything were to happen, I knew it was my responsibility to make sure she got the care that she needed. I look back on those days fondly, and I am thankful that I could be there for her.

THE JOURNEY

❦

While recovering from my surgery, I spent much time reading my Living Bible. I was not smoking, and I had no desire to do so. Feeling better each day, I was praying and getting to know the Lord, though I had not yet returned to the church.

When Deede's twins were born, I was very emotional. Elated and in love with her baby boys, I felt a renewed sense of joy as I had at Deede's birth.

The afternoon before they were born, Deede was admitted to the hospital for Preeclampsia, and the delivery was induced a month early.

My sister had gone through her pregnancy calmly, knowing early on that she would likely require a C-section in the delivery process. To Deede's mind, the birth would happen under anesthesia with no birthing pains. However, after admission to the hospital and an ultrasound, one of the babies had flipped positions and was ready to be born. In that moment, I could tell that my sister was frightened. Although she was concerned about what would happen next, and I sympathized with her fear, I still could not help but feel jealous of her. Despite all she had gone through, I still wished it were me.

At approximately 7 am, my sister was in an operating room just in case the C-section became necessary. It just so happened that an old friend of ours was the circulating nurse that night. Thankfully, she kept us informed about the progress of things. At one point, the nurse came out to tell us that Deede was ready and the first baby would be born soon. Not long after the nurse came out, we heard the news—my sister's first child had arrived! 6lbs 3oz, and completely healthy. I was so excited to meet him. At first, we believed that the second twin would be born immediately. We were quickly informed that it could be hours and perhaps even days before we saw the next baby. Thankfully, my sister did not have to wait that long. Two hours later, her second son was born.

It was some time before the twins were brought out to the waiting room for us to see, but when they did, I fell in love with them instantly. Tyler was wrinkled, with a quiet look and open eyes. Taylor's head wasn't quite round due to the difficulties surrounding his delivery. We all felt very blessed. My sister was a trooper throughout labor and delivery. Our lives were forever changed that day.

The boys were born on Thursday, May 31, 1990. Mom and Shannon decided to go to the hospital to be with Deede and the babies, then leave afterward to go to work in the evening. On Saturday, June 2, 1990, I was working as a waitress when the sky became dark and eerie-looking. The wind became fierce, and everything felt ominous. Mom and Shannon were at the hospital with Deede and the 2-day-old babies when they were told all visitors had to leave the hospital in anticipation of a storm moving in. Shortly thereafter, tornado sirens began to wail. Unknown to us, Deede had been given her babies by the hospital staff, and they had moved into the hallway. Alone and frightened, they waited as tornadoes moved through our area. I was terrified, wondering if they were okay. Had the hospital been hit? Were Mom and Shannon still there, or had they made it to work? Reports began to come in about heavy damage just south of our city. There was great devastation, but the hospital was safe. Thank the Lord for answering my desperate prayers that day!

The months following were busy with the twins. Deede and the babies would continue to stay with me at night while Mom and Shannon continued to work the night shift. All summer, my desire for a child greatly increased. I went back on Clomid and again experienced side effects that were, at times, crippling. I continued to hold out hope that—due to the corrective surgery I had—a pregnancy was coming soon. Meanwhile, I continued to devour the Word of God. Every free moment was spent reading the Bible and coming to realize my desire to have a child was a godly desire, not selfish, but a plan from the very beginning of the world to go forth and multiply.

I learned of Eve's disobedience in the Garden of Eden and how it had brought painful childbirth into existence. I could not escape the continual thoughts of becoming a mother. As I continued to read the Living Bible, I felt the drawing of the Lord. I wanted to purchase a King James Version Bible and get deeper into Scripture. I was reading about Adam and Eve, their sons Cain and Abel, and Seth. I continued in the book of Genesis, and I discovered the story of Abraham and Sarah. Although it seemed impossible to them, they miraculously became pregnant in their old age! God could open a womb that seemed dead. Reading that story revived my hopes of having a child of my own.

I had always gone to church, and I had some understanding of biblical stories. Our mother had always made a way for us to go to Sunday School. She would even arrange for a church bus to transport us. She told us stories about miraculous healings she had witnessed as a child, and she would never let us use the Lord's name in vain.

Even though my mom did not actively serve God, she believed the Bible and taught us to do the same. Mom assured us that, one day, she would serve Him, and eventually, she did just that. Our mother became a minister to the deaf and hearing impaired. She believed that everyone needed to hear about the love of Jesus. It was her mission to tell those who had not heard all she could tell them about her Lord and Savior, Jesus Christ. Mother earned two degrees in theology, and she became a licensed minister at the age of sixty. I was so proud of her. Her life became a witness to so many others.

My maternal Grandfather was a devout Nazarene Preacher, and my paternal Grandfather was an elder in the Baptist Church and a Gideon. But the ones who spiritually influenced me the most were my stepfather's parents, Mamaw and Papaw Meadows. The Meadows were Apostolic Pentecostals and faithful servants of the

Most High God. Mamaw had a soft spot for me, and she would often invite me over for the weekend to shop and play board games on Saturday. Then, I would go to church with her on Sunday. Mamaw would answer my questions about the church and tell me about the rapture—the catching away of the saints. When I look back, I cherish the days I spent with them and the things of God that they instilled in me. As God would have it, we now attend the church that they helped build in the 1980's. I have often wondered how many nails my Papaw might have hammered in or which walls and floors Mamaw might have come to clean. They always spoke of working at the church during its construction and that they spent every evening after work helping in any way they could until it was finished.

༄

On Thursday, August 2, 1990, Iraq invaded Kuwait. I was terrified, and I believed that invasion was the beginning of the end of times. I was so stirred up that I read the entire book of Revelation in one sitting. I didn't understand much of what I read, but it did say that Jesus is God and that He is the "Alpha and the Omega" and the "Beginning and the End." I believed what I was reading, and I wanted to know Him more intimately than I had in the past. Above all else, I wanted to be saved. This marked the beginning of my desire to be baptized in Jesus' name and to be filled with the gift of the Holy Ghost. I could not wait to get back to church on Sunday morning. I began faithfully attending church that weekend, and I continue to do so to this day.

That same year, my doctor put me back on Clomid, but it made me very sick. While on the medication, my mind became a total fog. It felt like I was walking in a dream sequence every waking hour. It was like nothing was real, everything was strange, and nothing felt right. I was experiencing mood swings, psychological side effects, visual disturbances, and increased ovarian cyst formation.

In short—everything that could go wrong with the medication was going wrong all at once. Due to the side effects, the doctor decided that it was best to stop the medication. Although the medicine caused me a great deal of pain, I was devastated. Instead, we would just continue to hope that my surgery had been successful and perhaps I would soon become pregnant.

☙

On August 28, 1990, during a revival service at our church, I received the precious, life-changing gift of the Holy Ghost. To that point, I had been attending every service for the month, but on that night, something was different. We were in the second night of revival, and the speaker was fiery. Looking back, I can recall that the musicians and singers seemed to be filled with the same passion and fervor as the preacher. I felt the presence of the Lord in a brand-new way, and there was no doubt in my mind the Lord was among us. I could not wait to get to the altar.

At the first mention of the call, I ran to the front of the church, my hands in the air in complete and total surrender to the God of all creation. I was filled with the Holy Ghost and began to speak in other tongues. I was reborn! I knew I was different, changed, and a brand-new creature. I could feel Jesus living on the inside of me, and I was immediately baptized in Jesus' name.

The next morning, I was in my second week at a new job. I left the restaurant for a cashier position and was fortunate to be employed closer to home. On that morning, a man I had never met before walked into the store, stopped, looked at me, pointed his finger, and said, "He who has begun a good work in you will perfect it to the day of Christ Jesus our Lord." I asked why he spoke that to me, and he answered that, as he was walking past me, the Lord had told him to. I shared with the man that I had received the Holy Ghost the night before and that I was stunned that he had just spoken these words to me. We began a friendship that would last until he passed away almost twenty-seven years later. He and his wife became my mentors and friends. In fact, they were more than friends—they became my family. His name was Jim, and he asked me if I was receiving home bible studies or not. I was not, so he spent months coming to our home every Monday evening to teach me and my unsaved husband the word of God. Looking back, those were special times of breaking the bread of life together.

During this great change in my spiritual life, I was recovering from having stopped the Clomid at the first of the month. It was as though I could now see the world from a beautiful new perspective. Just as the Scripture says in 2 Corinthians 5:17...

> *Therefore if any man be in Christ, he is a new creature: old things are passed away; behold, all things are become new.*

I was living that Scripture in every way imaginable. We were entering the fall season, and as the leaves began to change and the mums and pumpkins emerged, everything was different, vibrant, and new. In short, I was elated, and I was filled with new hope.

I could not get enough of the Word, of preaching, or of fellowship with like-minded believers. I would go to neighboring churches for revivals or alternate services. At one point, Brother Jim's church was having a service, and he invited us to come. I decided to go. At the beginning of that service, I was sitting in the back row, and I could feel God's presence so near. I asked the Lord to give me a sign that it was Him, as I was new to my walk with God and still had so many questions. I said, "Lord, if this is you, let that woman on the front row come back and pray for me." Within seconds, that specific woman came to the back and asked if she could pray for me. Of course, I said yes. Much like Jim, that woman eventually became one of my dearest friends. Her name was Aleatha, and she was to soon become Brother Jim's wife.

I would sit and ponder all the things the Lord had done so many times to prove Himself to me. How could He love me so much?

Desert Storm was ramping up during that time, and my baby brother Rick (no longer Ricky), was now 24 and serving in the United States Navy. He was stationed in the Persian Gulf during the war, and my mother and I were a nervous wreck. I leaned on the Lord through prayer and asked Him to watch over and protect our soldiers and my younger brother.

I was concerned not only for Rick's safety but for his salvation. I began writing him letters and soon learned that there were restrictions on what materials of a Christian nature could be sent to soldiers and sailors from back home. I would write to Rick a few times per week, sharing with him scriptures I had discovered. I would tell him where I was reading in the Bible, and I shared with him recaps of sermons I was hearing, all the while praying earnestly that somehow, he could get a Bible into his hands.

There were no emails or texts at that time, and I received a letter back from Rick long after he had sent it to me. Rick's letter said that the Gideons had boarded the ship the day before and given them all Bibles! I was overwhelmed with gratitude that the Lord had answered my prayer of putting a bible into Rick's hands. Now, we could share with one another what we were discovering in the Word of God. That was another faith-builder for me, teaching me to trust in the Lord and believe that He hears and answers prayers.

☙

February 18, 1991, was a day that will forever be etched into my memory. It had been six months since I received the gift of the Holy Ghost, and the Lord was repeatedly showing me ways He could be trusted and proven. For three days, I had been incredibly burdened for my brother in the Persian Gulf. Though he was not on land, missiles fired from Iraq were being intercepted by ships in the Gulf, exactly where my brother was serving. I was praying for him night and day. I would wake up in the night, crawl out of bed, kneel in the dark, and cry out to God to protect Rick.

That Friday, Saturday, and Sunday were filled with prayers for him, and I could not get out from underneath the worry and heaviness. I had not yet learned in my early walk what it meant to intercede for someone or to travail in prayer, though I now understand that is what I was doing. Finally, on Sunday evening, in a ladies' prayer room before our weekly service, a dear sister came to me in the dimly lit room with others and said to me the Lord had impressed upon her to pray for my brother and that he would be protected by the Holy Spirit and His angels. We joined hands and hearts as we prayed for Rick. Suddenly, the burden and heaviness were gone, and I felt peace and a sense of relief. I went home and was able to sleep soundly for the first time in three nights.

I went to work the next day and, as part of my routine, turned on the TV to wait for the local news at 5 pm. Immediately, there was a newsbreak. On the "Upcoming News," a U.S. boat had hit a floating mine in the Persian Gulf with reports of three American casualties on board. I went to my knees right there and began crying out to God, "Please God, don't let it be Rick! But Lord, someone's child has perished, and please bring comfort to those who have lost." It seemed like it was an eternity before the news identified the name of the ship. It was the USS Princeton—not the ship my brother was on. I was relieved, but only for a moment. I began to feel sad for the ones whose loved ones were lost that day. I began to pray for the families involved, but I thanked the Lord over and over for caring for Rick.

A few years later, Rick and I were talking about his time in the Gulf, and I shared this particular story. I told Rick about my burden and the prayers. Rick asked me to repeat what and when I was praying. He told me that their ship was initially en route to the same place as the USS Princeton attack, but they were surprisingly turned around instead. Had they continued on their course, it may have been their ship, a smaller vessel, that would have hit that mine instead, likely suffering much more damage and loss of life. Surely, the Lord had answered my prayers.

On February 23, 1991, our pastor called an urgent prayer meeting. The news was reporting air strikes that had been going on in Iraq was transitioning to a ground war that would begin within the next 24 hours. Many of us gathered at the church, seeking the Lord for the protection of our soldiers and innocent Iraqis. My brother was on a ship but still in danger. I prayed fervently, and I asked the others to remember my brother in their prayers. I continued to write to Rick regularly. I sent him books about Bible heroes, and he said that he most enjoyed *John: Son of Thunder* by Ellen Gunderson Traylor. I can recall how when Rick was a young boy, he loved the Lord, and he was a member of The Royal Rangers youth program at our local Assembly of God church. Rick would put on a necktie with his tee shirt, grab a Bible, stand on the living room coffee table, and preach his heart out. He had a call from God on his life from a young age. I believe he still does.

While burdened for Rick in the Persian Gulf, I was watching my sister at home learn how to be a young mother of twins. The boys had different personalities—Tyler was quiet and somber, and he didn't fuss at all unless he truly needed something. But Taylor was rarely quiet and very busy. My sister allowed me to have them on Saturday nights so that I could take them to Sunday School. Being with the boys allowed me to experience a small taste of what motherhood was like, which was both soul-soothing and painful for me.

THE JOURNEY

One morning, in the parking lot of my church, I sat with the boys, and I committed them to the Lord. I asked the Lord to watch over them, keep them safe, bless them with health, a joyful childhood, and parents who would remain together and raise them without separation. I prayed that the boys would always know and love the Lord. At that time, I was the only one in our family who was a born-again believer. It was my mission to pray for the salvation of each one of them. I wanted everyone to know that wonderful Jesus who was now the center of my being.

☙

In April, one year after my major surgery, my doctor was concerned that I had not yet conceived. A second Hysterosalpingogram was ordered. The result was not good news, and the conclusion was that the adhesions removed in the first surgery had returned.

The doctor looked at me, and he said that there was no longer any chance for me to conceive a child. Physically, it was impossible. When I heard those words, the hard metal table that I was lying on felt so cold. My world imploded, and it felt as though things were falling apart. My doctor conveyed his sympathies, but as I laid on the table, I began to cry.

"God, where are you? What is next? How do I move forward?"

Heaven seemed silent. I managed to get dressed and head to my car. Once in my car, I wept again. After a while,

I gathered myself together and drove home. I began to consider all that had recently transpired in life. I had been attending so many prayer meetings. God had been showing himself to me. He had proven Himself to be mighty and powerful when He protected my brother from that attack. Surely, God would also prove how mighty He was by giving me the gift of conception. Somehow, it had to happen. I wondered to myself if it would happen for me like it did for Sarah in the Bible. Would I conceive when I was much older? I was searching for hope and answers. I knew God alone held both.

There were times when my faith wavered. During those times, I would allow my mind to become the devil's playground. I entertained thoughts like, "I can't have children because I am too heavy," or, "I can't have children because I had been such a bad person." I convinced myself that my DNA was such a mistake that God would not allow my DNA to continue. I wondered if I could not be a mother because I would not be a good parent. Still, I remembered that the Bible said our thoughts should be captivated by Christ, not our worries. I would get my Bible out and begin reading the book of Psalms to encourage myself. I would listen to Gospel music and preaching tapes and get lost in God's Word. Those were the things that got me through the hardest days.

The twins began crawling, walking, and talking. In many ways, they were the salve to my hurting heart. I would look at them and long to have children of my own.

My sister and brother-in-law never once told me "no" when I asked to watch them. They allowed me to take the boys every year on the eve of Thanksgiving. It was our tradition to have the twins pick what they wanted to eat, and then I would prepare it for them and show them how to make it. Because of our Thanksgiving-Eve tradition, at five years old, Taylor could properly crimp a pie crust. Opposites in personality, the boys remained a bright spot during a dark season of my life.

One weekend, when the twins were with me, I watched them playing outside with my husband. I began to pray and thank the Lord for them, telling God that I did not know love like the love I had for my nephews was possible. The Lord responded to me in that moment and said, "I love you like that and more." I could not comprehend the depth of His love for me. How could God love me more than I loved those boys?

Our Monday night Bible studies continued, and Brother Jim was a faithful and relatable teacher who became a dear friend. My husband did not go to church and did not have any desire to do so. Still, he allowed Bible studies to continue in our home and even participated in them. The Word was being spoken in my house, and I knew God was near to me, even in my distress.

One day, Brother Jim came to my place of employment. He shared with me that he was now engaged to be married!

I responded, "Oh, please tell me it's that beautiful girl who came and prayed for me when I visited your church!" It was indeed. Both Brother Jim and Sister Aleatha had contributed so much to my spiritual life, so, as far as I was concerned, they were perfectly matched. She had spoken into my life for years, and I had learned so much from her. They married on New Year's Day, and together, they became a powerful ministry team.

My own marriage was not healthy, and I had changed in many ways after becoming a Christian. My husband was supportive of me, but things were different. I lived a life of church services and seeking an ever-growing relationship with Jesus. My husband did not. At the same time, I was not feeling settled in my church anymore, and I was grieving my inability to conceive. Things were difficult at home, and eventually, I stopped attending church for nearly a full year. While angry with God for not giving me the things I wanted, I was also too afraid to take my anger and hurt feelings to Him in prayer. Instead, I hung my head in shame and avoided talking with the Lord. I became miserable. Over time, I longed to return to the church, but I avoided phone calls from Brother Jim, and anyone associated with the church out of shame. I was trying to outrun the pain I was feeling from the dissatisfaction in my life.

It can be difficult to explain to people how my desires shaped my focus in the present. It seemed that most days, I would turn on the TV and there were stories of tragedies happening to children. Commercials would appear late at night asking for monthly support for hungry children. In some ways, it felt as though they were haunting me.

Physically, I was still suffering during this time as well. My menstrual cycles were increasingly painful, heavy, and completely unpredictable. I would menstruate for weeks on end, on two occasions requiring a D&C procedure to go into surgery to have the lining of my uterus scraped to stop the sloughing of it, thereby stopping the bleeding that had been going on for weeks, causing pain, cramping, and anemia. Some days I felt I was drowning in a deep hole that I could not escape. Nevertheless, I knew God had not left me. Over the course of that year, I was away from the church, and I could hear a voice speaking to my heart, telling me to get back to the church and return to fellowship with God. I knew it was the answer, but I felt as though I would have to spiritually regain ground that had been lost while I was away.

One evening, I picked up my Bible and held it up to God. It had been several months since I had read my Bible, but this time was a bit different. I said out loud, "Lord, if you are real, and if you see me in my pain, let me know. Please speak to me in your Word." Challenging God to speak to me in a miraculous way, I then let the Bible fall open. Whatever it said, it would say. And as the cover opened and the pages spread, this is the passage that was sitting in front of me:

> *I have blotted out, as a thick cloud, thy transgressions, and, as a cloud, thy sins: RETURN UNTO ME; for I have redeemed thee.* — Isaiah 44:22, emphasis added

In that moment, I knew that the God of heaven had again heard me, and He was indeed proving Himself to me. I knew I had to trust in Him and, in making my way back to the house of God, dwell with Him again.

One evening, not long after, I went to a local department store to do some Christmas shopping. On the way out of the store, I heard someone calling to me from the dark parking lot. I turned to see a lovely couple whom I recognized from my time at the church. Of course, I do not believe it was any coincidence that I had run into them on that day during that season of my life. Recently, God had spoken to me and told me to return to Him. Now, He was giving me the opportunity to do so. The couple came up to me, and the wife said she was so glad to see me and that she had been praying fervently for me. The sister had been in the church for many years, and she had a keen sense of discernment. She looked me right In the eye and said, "You haven't been going to church, have you?" I told her that I had not, but I was also confused. I was certain that the woman must have been aware of my absence from the church over the course of the year. Then she told me that she and her husband had begun pastoring a small church nearby and were no longer at the church we had attended together.

THE JOURNEY

 I asked her if she would mind if I were to visit their church, and she told me I should consider returning to the church we had attended together first. When I explained to her that I had made the decision not to go back, she and her husband said they would welcome me at their church if that is what it would take to get me back to the house of God.

☙

Looking back on those days, I know that couple was a lifeline sent by God to rescue me. Two days later, I attended church for the first time in over ten months. I remained faithful in my attendance, and for a year and a half, I sat under their ministry. Allowing the Lord to teach me more Scripture and grow in understanding, I shared with them my desire to have children. I also told them about the emotional and physical toll the last year had taken on me.

 After my year and a half with that couple, it was time for me to move forward in my walk with God once again. Knowing that I would not stay there, I began seeking God and asking Him where I should put down roots. I was in love with my Lord again, and I was determined to find a church to call home and remain faithful to Him forever.

 I knew I needed to be connected to a church where I could remain involved and serve. The Lord led me to a nearby church where some people I knew attended. They welcomed me with open arms, and I knew it was the place I was supposed to be.

Other than a mother, the only thing I had ever wanted to become was a nurse. The Lord made a way for me to return to school, and I began focusing my energy on earning a nursing degree. During nursing school, we had clinicals in several different medical disciplines, and there were days we worked on both the pediatric units and the labor and delivery units. Those were excruciatingly painful rotations for me, solidifying my resolve to never work on either. I could not handle seeing pregnant women, childbirth, new babies, or small children. It was like pouring salt into open wounds, and I could hardly bear it.

Nursing graduation came, and I was honored to give our class speech. I was settled into my new church, where Brother Jim and Sister Aleatha had been members for a long time. The church was busy, and I felt that I was healing. It was a fiery church with exuberant worship and earnest preaching. I felt renewed. I began making friends and getting to know the members. I attended weekly Friday morning prayer meetings, all scheduled services, and eventually began teaching a spiritually-based weight loss class. I was honored to be asked to be part of the outreach department, teaching home bible studies and organizing events. I was also participating in hospitality by preparing meals and helping with other needs. I loved my church and my church family. Over time, I began to share my struggles with infertility with Jim and Aleatha. Remembering the story of Hannah and her son Samuel, I prayed Hannah's prayer often. The Bible says that God is not a respecter of persons, so what He has done for one, He can do for all. I believed I could be like Hannah and Sarah, and, in God's time, perhaps I would.

CHAPTER 3

A Mother's Day Promise

May 12, 1996, Mother's Day, was a monumental day for me. I received a promise from God that day—a promise I could have confidence in, knowing that God was able to finish the work that He started. That morning at the church was all about mothers. No way to escape the feelings of the day—the loss of not being a mother—I prepared myself to endure the weekend. I had been prayerful for weeks, knowing this day was coming, and I was handling the day and my emotions fairly well. After Sunday morning services, my mom, sister, and all the family were at my home for Sunday dinner. I invited everyone to come to the evening service with me, but the only one who agreed was my young stepbrother, John.

At the beginning of the evening service, as the music began to play, I felt a tug at my heart, not a tug of sadness, but of gratitude for my own mother. I felt gratitude for my sister and for what a tremendous mother she had turned out to be, and gratitude for a good day with family. I felt a sense of worship welling up in my heart and began to move to the altar as others in the congregation did the same. I asked John if he wanted to come with me, and he said no. As I neared the altar, I felt God speak to me and urge me to talk to Him about my desire to become a mother. I stopped in my tracks still a few feet from the altar and whispered, "No Lord, I cannot talk about this, not today."

As I stood still, the drawing of the Lord was so profound that I could not resist. I walked the few remaining steps to the front of the church and began to weep. I opened my heart completely, something I had not done in a very long time. I was open to hear what the Lord would say to me. For the most part, I had closed off this subject in my prayer time. I believed I was unworthy of motherhood, so I began focusing on my new nursing career, caring for my sister's twins, and hiding my pain from the Lord. But it is not possible to hide anything from God. We can, however, resist Him, and I was choosing not to discuss my pain. I believed He was able to answer but I also believed I was unworthy to receive.

As I began to let my guard down, I could feel the Lord's presence surround me. My heart began to cry, and I poured out to God my desire to be a mother. I allowed Him into a place I had reserved for only myself. The Lord told me that He heard my cries even when they were silent and buried deep inside. He told me that He knows my desire and He has the answer. Finally, God spoke to me and said this:

"A pregnancy will come with much affliction. Are you willing to endure?"

I stood quietly for a few moments before responding with these words: "Lord, if you will walk with me, I can endure anything. I will accept the affliction if you allow me to become a mother." As clearly as I have ever heard the Lord speak—nearly audibly—He said, "It shall be."

In that moment it was as if I had new life breathed into me. I opened my eyes to see many people around me praying with and for me. Immediately, Brother Jim, now our assistant pastor, looked me in the eye and said, "It shall be." I was stunned at his choice of words.

I asked, "Why did you say those words?"

His answer: because the Lord told him to do so. He then said, "Look to your right."

I looked, and there was my 14-year-old stepbrother, hands lifted high, tears streaming down his face, receiving the precious life-changing gift of the Holy Ghost. I was ecstatic. What had just transpired here? New life in John, new hope in me, and a promise that I would conceive? I had heard the voice of God, and nothing would ever convince me to not believe. I knew I was destined to become a mother. Joy unspeakable filled my soul! As the service ended, there had been so much prayer that the Pastor dismissed service, saying there was not a message he could deliver to compare to what the Lord had just accomplished. I walked to the back pew where sister Aleatha had been praying with someone, and she said I was simply glowing. Hope had been renewed. I left feeling restored, and I hurried home to share the news with my husband, my mother, and my sister.

Soon after the life-changing service, Aleatha gifted me a Noah's Ark statue, saying she was agreeing with me in prayer for the fulfillment of my promise. Just as Noah had a promise that God would never destroy the earth by water again, I had a promise from God that I would indeed be a mother. I was filled with joyous expectation, the definition of the word "hope" in many Bible translations. I was standing on the words of Hebrews 11:1...

> *Now faith is the substance of things hoped for, the evidence of things not seen.*

I could not see what God was doing, but I was confident in His promise and would be content in the waiting.

Just as Noah built the ark with only a word from God but no tangible proof of coming rain, I began to prepare a nursery in my home by faith. We had an extra bedroom we called our office; it would be perfect. I began to pray about the room, the theme, and consider what would come. We purchased a rocking chair and a dresser, and we decorated in the theme of Noah's ark. God keeps His promises. Those were words I would live on.

Days passed, and the weeks became months with no natural pregnancy. My husband and I decided it was time to move forward with medical intervention. We met with my gynecologist for guidance; perhaps in vitro fertilization was the answer? We needed more information. We attempted to become licensed foster parents, but the thought of reunification and the loss that it could create for us was too much. I was not in an emotional place where I could open my home to a child who might not stay.

For the second time, my doctor asked me to consider in vitro fertilization. At the very least, he asked that I contact the fertility specialists in my state and have a consultation. My husband and I agreed, and I made an appointment to attend a seminar at their offices two hours away. We attended an informational presentation one evening to learn more. It was emotional, but it was an experience that renewed my hope that my husband and I could conceive. I wondered, "Was this the way the Lord would answer our prayers?" We began the process that evening. After making a commitment and an appointment, I went to prayer, and I opened my heart to the Lord, asking Him to walk with us through the process while vividly remembering His promise that a pregnancy would come with much affliction. I was ready.

While praying the night before our first appointment to officially begin the process, I was kneeling at our living room sofa when I again heard the Lord speak to me: "Are you willing to suffer loss along the way?" Yes, Lord, if loss is your will, I trust you. I will accept the loss. I had no idea what that meant. Would I have a child who would die? Would I lose friends? Would we move away? What loss could God be speaking of? It did not matter to me at the time. Whatever it took, I was willing to endure absolutely anything.

Our first appointment and task was to begin the medications to stimulate ovulation for the next step of harvesting the eggs. I began Lupron injections daily. I was comfortable with self-administering the medication and felt grateful for each injection as it was bringing me one step closer to pregnancy. An exciting season of anticipation and hope had begun. I was quick to research Lupron, why this was the medication of choice, learning how it worked on the hormones, causing the brain in the area of the hypothalamus to stimulate the hormone called GnRH, which would cause stimulation of another part of the brain called the pituitary which would release FSH and LH in the blood which would ultimately cause the ovaries to grow an egg, produce estrogen and ovulate. I did have some side effects: immediate weight gain, hot flashes, headaches, and joint pain. Every ache and pain was worth it, and nothing would deter me.

I was having frequent blood work, and then, when indicated, began progesterone oil injections—they were brutal. These were also daily injections but were given in the hip, rotating the site daily. This medication is in an oil preparation—thick with a large bore needle, and quite painful. Both hips were incredibly bruised, my husband did not feel comfortable giving the injections, and I could not self-administer, so dear Sister Aleatha would give them each evening. Progesterone prepares the uterine lining to receive the fertilized egg/eggs and would continue for at least a few weeks into the pregnancy to ensure a healthy environment for the babies in which to grow. I kept all the used needles in a large glass jar to hopefully, one day, show our children the cost of IVF and the value of enduring difficulty in order to bring them into the world.

The needles were a tangible sign of what was yet to come.

My body changed during treatment. My abdominal bloating was noticeable, and my clothing felt tight. Some weight gain was happening, and my appetite was ravenous. I also felt fatigued and found myself napping daily. Daily blood draws were necessary to monitor hormone levels. Finally, they had reached the optimum level. Egg retrieval would be on Monday, June 30. Everything was going smoothly. We were scheduled to arrive that morning at 9 am. The anticipation was at the highest level I had ever known. My husband had to be admitted into the hospital as an outpatient with me as he would have to provide a fresh sperm sample for fertilization. He would do that as my eggs were being retrieved, and we would come together following the procedure. I was sedated during the retrieval. Retrieval is done by a needle being passed through the vaginal wall under ultrasound guidance to the ovaries. The needle is connected to a device using suction and a test tube. The physician would retrieve the egg by inserting the needle into a follicle, pulling the egg and the surrounding fluid into the needle, and then into the test tube. The eggs are then taken to the lab and combined with the sperm to hopefully accept fertilization.

I had a short recovery from anesthesia and was instructed to go home, take it easy, continue injections, and expect a call with an update on when to return in the next 3-5 days for embryo transfer. It was surreal in so many ways.

I had been studying the word of God for seven years and had many scriptures that brought me much comfort in this area of my life. There had been times when I literally thought I would lose my sanity in my pursuit of motherhood. Times when I would believe every negative word ever spoken over me or every negative thought that would enter my mind. It was tormenting. I would return to the Word of God and ask him to guard my heart and my mind as according to His Word in Philippians 4:6-7. It was only by the grace of God that I did not spiral. I would ask the Lord to help me bring my thoughts captive unto the mind of Christ, casting down my own imaginations telling me I was less than, not a whole woman, I was broken, due to being barren. 2 Corinthians 10:5 helped when those days would come.

A MOTHER'S DAY PROMISE

> *Casting down imaginations, and every high thing that exalteth itself against the knowledge of God, and bringing into captivity every thought to the obedience of Christ;* — 2 Corinthians 10:5

That evening around bedtime, the lab called to tell me that four of my eggs had accepted fertilization and had active cell division.

"Four," I thought to myself. Our minds could hardly begin to comprehend.

We had agreed to allow the fertilization of all the eggs and not to do any cryopreservation. It was a hard decision, but it was one we felt was best for us and our beliefs. We had also agreed that if all four accepted fertilization, we would not "selectively reduce" or remove two of the four or any amount that had accepted fertilization. Once the cell division began, life had happened. Only God could decide how many would survive to birth.

The next morning the 4 cells were now 16 and 32. Two of each, all were continuing to divide and grow. We received a phone call each morning and each evening with updates on current cell count and division. All four were continuing successfully, and embryo transfer would be on Friday, July 4.

For the transfer, My mother accompanied my husband and I to the hospital two hours north of where we lived. My mother placed pillows and blankets in the back of her SUV for me to lay on for the return ride home. The drive home was full of hope and anticipation. We were on our way to having four children! How would we ever manage quadruplets?

I returned on Monday, July 7 for bloodwork. My HCG levels were rising, indicative of a positive pregnancy.

☙

While reading my Bible, the Lord took me to Isaiah 54:1. This Scripture puzzled me, but it gave me hope at the same time. It was a strange feeling.

> *Sing, O barren, thou that didst not bear, break forth into singing, and cry aloud, thou that didst not travail with child: for more are the children of the desolate than the children of the married wife, saith the Lord.* — Isaiah 54:1

I had been serving the Lord long enough to know when He was speaking to me. Why, with as much study as I had done, had I not realized this Scripture before? Why now, during IVF, was I feeling God bring this to me and show me words that say "barren" and, "that did not travail with child?" What did it mean? I pondered these words in my heart.

I was feeling happy, and I bought a few baby blankets. With quadruplets on the way, I would require many of them. My family was supportive but cautious. They were concerned about possibilities I had refused to entertain.

I returned to the hospital on Friday, one week after the transfer. Now, my HCG levels were not rising as quickly as they should be. I was told not to worry and that it could be a sign that only one or two of the babies had implanted. Potentially, none of them had at all. That brought me great sadness as I knew life had taken place with the cell division and acceptance of fertilization, so if less than four were now viable, we had lost a child or possibly children. I was heartbroken by that news because it meant that I had essentially had a miscarriage. There was a new sadness creeping in that I could not succumb to until I knew for sure.

On Monday morning, it had been ten days since the transfer. I woke up with the familiar feeling of lower back pain, cramps, and the overall feeling of unwellness. I thought to myself, "Please God, no. Not loss—please, I cannot lose these babies."

I did the only thing I knew to do. I got into my car and went to the church to pray. I called the doctor's office. I already had an appointment for the next morning, and I wanted some reassurance that the next ultrasound would show that all was well. In my heart, I knew that was likely not the case.

When I got to the church, I went into the sanctuary and walked behind the platform by the baptismal changing room. I knelt and began to pray and seek comfort for what I was beginning to understand was happening inside of me. I knew my body, and it was clear to me that I was miscarrying the quadruplets. I was afraid of those thoughts —it made me feel as though I were lacking faith. The truth is, I was desperately holding onto faith. This was the way I was to become a mother, right? As I began to cry out to God in my heartache and fear, His presence overwhelmed me. He was near and offering comfort.

The Lord whispered into my spirit, "I am the God of Abraham, Isaac and Jacob. I will not leave you in a desert place." I did not fully understand the significance of those words, but I knew the storm was coming, and He was with me.

I prayed and sobbed for some time, then I got up with the resolve to face and accept the loss of the babies. Feelings of death and comfort were co-existing in my heart. I did not fully understand it, but I was going to trust in the Lord no matter what.

As I stepped out of the sanctuary, I noticed Brother Jim and Sister Aleatha. They saw me and spoke to me for a while about all that had transpired. I asked if I could share with them what had just taken place in prayer. Of course, they said yes.

As I repeated to them what the Lord had said, Sis Aleatha said, "Sharon, all three of those men had barren wives. All three of the wives eventually became mothers. If this pregnancy does not continue, you have a promise from God that a pregnancy would come with much affliction, and you now have His word that He will not leave you in a desert place. He will never leave you in a dry and thirsty land. Hold onto his words and allow Him to comfort you."

Those words became my comfort as I awakened the following morning with bleeding, pain, and cramps. The doctor's appointment included labs ordered stat, I would go home and await results before scheduling an ultrasound and further care.

I received the dreaded phone call approximately 2 hours later—the pregnancy was lost. I was devastated.

I hung up the phone and walked out my back door, falling on the ground in emotional upheaval. I wailed for a long time. Eventually, my husband came outside to get me up and into the house.

I was in a place I had never been before. The loss was great, and I felt as if I were swimming in an area as vast as the ocean. I had no lifeline—no way to come up for air. How was I supposed to keep going on?

To his great credit, my husband did all he could to comfort me. He called the church and my mother. My mother left work and immediately came to my home. Mom walked into my bedroom and looked at me. She tried to hold me, but I did not want anyone to touch me. There was no place of comfort. Nothing could be said or done to ease the intensity of my pain. Nothing. Mother said things from her heart, and I know she was searching for a way to ease my torment. When she said, "I know how you feel," it drove me absolutely crazy. She did not know how I felt because she had three children of her own. I asked her to leave. Looking back on that time, I regret not allowing her to comfort me during my darkest days. I was not in a stable mindset, and although I know she understood and forgave me for my outburst, I wish I could have received what she was trying to give. As the saying goes, "Hurt people, hurt people." I was hurting as never before.

I remained in bed all that day and the next. The following day, Thursday, our church was beginning our annual revival with our speaker who was young and vibrant and in tune with the Lord. We looked forward to this time every year. Nevertheless, I decided I would not go to the revival. Perhaps I would never go to church again. I knew that it was wrong to consider abandoning church. Still, try as I might, I couldn't shake the thought that my days with the church were numbered. Later that afternoon, Brother Jim called me again. He had been calling me consistently for two days, but I had been refusing all his calls. At the urging of my husband, I finally agreed to talk to him. While he sympathized with my feelings, Jim pleaded with me not to allow anger to keep me out of the presence of God. Jim encouraged me to find a place to pray and to let God have all of the burdens I was carrying—even the anger. Yes, I was angry at God. After all, I had spent my life believing one thing only to be left with something else. Jim said if I didn't give it all to God, I would die spiritually and never recover. At those words, I hung up on him.

The time for our next church service was drawing near. I asked my husband if he would accompany me to this service, and he agreed. Because I did not want to speak to anyone about all that had transpired, we arrived just after service began. No sooner did we sit down than one of the sisters came and asked if she could pray for me. I responded adamantly with a no. The sister was persistent, and I couldn't handle it. Because of the incident, my husband asked if I was ready to leave. I grabbed my purse and Bible, and we left through the back door. As we were beginning to back out of the parking space, a younger sister in Christ came to my window. She said she had no idea what was wrong but asked that I please not leave. She went on to say how I was a lifeline to her, and if I were to leave and not come back it would greatly affect her life. The motherly instincts in me responded to this woman's request. It brought me to tears. I looked at the pleading in her eyes, and I told her to give me a moment and agreed that I would come back inside. God bless that woman. I know if I had left that parking lot, I would have likely never gone back.

As my husband and I returned into the sanctuary of the church, our pastor stopped the service and asked that we come to the front of the sanctuary to be prayed over. He tactfully told the congregation that I had lost the quadruplets and needed space and time to heal. He asked that only the ministry pray over me that night, but in the days ahead, when I came to people's minds, to pray for me then. In short, he was asking the congregation to give the Lord His time to work. I was grateful for his words. And

I am also grateful to those who prayed for us during that time of loss.

It was a painful summer. I was trying to find purpose in my pain while not completely isolating myself from God, my husband, and others. I took a second job to help fill my time. When I was idle, I was sad. I had to stay busy.

☙

In 1998, I was contacted by one of the women in our church who knew of a baby that was being put up for adoption soon. We contacted the mother who was living in a homeless shelter with two other children at the time. We had a conversation, and it appeared she was interested in having us adopt the baby girl. We chose a name: Abigail Hope.

Abigail is my favorite woman in the Old Testament. She was brave, and the Bible says she was a woman of good understanding and had a beautiful countenance. When King David was ready to destroy her entire town because of the actions of her husband, Abigail stepped in to save her homeland. We decided on the name "Hope" because of the hope we have in Christ. Abigail Hope would be her name.

After a period of time, the mother of the unborn child stopped returning our phone calls. We were now experiencing a failed adoption. I felt as though I were missing the will of God yet again. Every time we got close to an answer, we hit a brick wall. The failed adoption was another painful disappointment to endure.

We found out several months later that the baby had been adopted by someone who went through a large adoption agency and had been born with Fetal Alcohol Syndrome, likely facing a lifetime of struggles. Her diagnosis would not have deterred us from adopting her, but I had to accept that the Lord had another plan.

∽

The ministry of our church took a trip to the Philippines. While in a service where over 5000 people were filled with the Holy Ghost, Brother Jim had a vision of a large angel standing over the arena where the crusade was taking place. He witnessed a goiter fall off a woman's neck during the service. He took his handkerchief out of his pocket and anointed it with oil. Jim had the ministers pray over that cloth and said to the Lord, "If you can heal here on this island as I have just witnessed, you can certainly heal Sharon's broken womb!" The handkerchief was given to me, and I carried it in my purse for years as a physical, tangible reminder and encouragement to pray that my promise would come true.

My menstrual cycles continued to be incredibly painful, and yearly exams were tough. I remember when I would arrive for my appointments, the office would always have pregnant women in the waiting room. I would look at them and smile if we made eye contact. But inside, I was screaming out in pain. Longing to participate in the joy they were experiencing right in front of me. During that time, I was overwhelmed by the feeling that there must be something wrong with me as a person. After all, why else would God reject me from being a mother?

Even in the pain, I continued to pursue God and my relationship with Him. I loved being a Christian, and I loved being part of my large church. I had come to know the pastor's daughter and our church secretary very well. It was now 1999, and I was still yearning for a child. The world was about to enter a new millennium. I was thirty-four years old, and I still did not have a child. My twin nephews were nine years old, and they were still the delight of our family. They often stayed weekends with me, and I cherished our close relationship. In many ways, they helped fill the gaping hole of motherhood in my life.

I continued to study the word of God. I discovered there were many more barren women in the Bible. Abraham, Isaac, and Jacob had barren wives. Hannah was barren. I kept reminding myself over and over as I read their stories that they had happy endings and that God proved himself faithful to each of them. Surely, He would prove faithful to me too.

In retrospect, I think I was trying to "earn" God's favor. If I were "good enough," if I "gave enough," "volunteered enough," on and on, maybe I would conceive.

I could not get away from Isaiah 54. God would continually take me to the chapter again and again, and I would read how the barren woman would break forth into singing. She would enlarge her tent to hold the blessings of those that her children would inherit. I asked myself, "How was the barren having seed?" Then, one day, after having read the chapter many times, verses 6-10 jumped from the page and into my spirit.

> *For the LORD hath called thee as a woman forsaken and grieved in spirit, and a wife of youth, when thou wast refused, saith thy God. For a small moment have I forsaken thee; but with great mercies will I gather thee. In a little wrath I hid my face from thee for a moment; but with everlasting kindness will I have mercy on thee, saith the LORD thy Redeemer. For this is as the waters of Noah unto me: for as I have sworn that the waters of Noah should no more go over the earth; so have I sworn that I would not be wroth with thee, nor rebuke thee. For the mountains shall depart, and the hills be removed; but my kindness shall not depart from thee, neither shall the covenant of my peace be removed, saith the LORD that hath mercy on thee.*

Then verse 13:

> *And all thy children shall be taught of the LORD; and great shall be the peace of thy children.*

These words repeatedly resounded in my mind and spirit. I questioned if it was truly the Lord. Was it just my strong desire to have children that was driving me? I would take that thought to prayer, every time feeling confident it was the Lord speaking to me. He was assuring me that I would parent. For a while, I felt hopeful. Then time would pass, the nursery would still be empty, the womb would ache, a baby would cry, and the pain would return. As had been the case so many times in my life, doubt was beginning to creep in.

Through it all, I was determined to never again turn away from the Lord. I loved Him, and I knew He had called me. He had proven Himself to me over and over, and He would not leave me in a desert place.

There was more about Isaiah 54 that was speaking to me at that time in my life:

> *No weapon that is formed against thee shall prosper; and every tongue that shall rise against thee in judgment thou shalt condemn. This is the heritage of the servants of the LORD, and their righteousness is of me, saith the LORD.*
> *— Isaiah 54:17*

I knew that being a mother was not wicked or ungodly. It is a desire I was born with, and it was created by God. He has a purpose for who I am and what I desire. I had to believe that God is not cruel, so when the weapons of my mind would come against me, I would not allow them to prosper. I would trust in God, His timing, and His plans.

A MOTHER'S DAY PROMISE

☙

In the year 2000, my birthday fell on both National Nurse's Day and Mother's Day.

I always dreaded the middle of April through Mother's Day. It was tortuous to me. One cannot get away from ads, radio announcements, church banquets, clothing sales, flowers; everything around you is announcing the special day when we honor mothers. It cannot be escaped.

That year was particularly painful since I was turning thirty-five years old, and my internal clock was ticking louder than ever before. I had been encouraging myself in the Lord for weeks, preparing for Sunday morning service honoring mothers. I thought I was prepared mentally to endure all of the celebration, until Mother's Day morning. I got up early, showered, dressed, and called my own mother to wish her a happy day. I was about to walk out the door for church when I decided to walk through the room we called the nursery. By faith, we had been decorating it. I knew I heard from God, and I held His promise close to me. I knew I would be a parent one day. As I entered our nursery, a wave of grief and sadness as I had never known hit me. It felt like a punch in the gut or a stab in the heart. All the pain from the loss of the quadruplets —all the times I had believed I was pregnant—only to feel that disappointment once again. All of the pain rushed in at once, like a tsunami. I had been having dreams of walking into this very room and seeing our child of promise.

I dreamed I would pick the baby up, hold her close, only to awaken to empty arms. I would sob myself back to a tormented sleep. I began to fear going to sleep because the dream state was now becoming as painful as the wake.

All at once, I fell to my knees and began to cry out to God. Knowing I could not face the day and would not be able to go to church, I prayed the most sincere prayer I had ever prayed. I once again began to tell God of the deep pain and the struggle of the emptiness in my womb. In my lowest state, I asked God to grant me this one request: If I could not be a mother by this same day next year, I asked the Lord to take my life.

Of course, this request was the product of a heavy and misguided heart. But I could not bear the pain again. It had become unbearable. I laid on the floor until the cries became a whimper. I somehow managed to get back into my room and crawl into bed. Almost catatonic, I stared at the ceiling as I laid there in agony. I spent the remainder of the morning in bed, staring and sitting with the ache in my heart. I was inconsolable for hours. I finally received a call from my assistant pastor, Brother Jim. He acknowledged my pain and encouraged me to talk to the Lord in prayer. I got up and went to see my Mother, but it was bittersweet. Thankfully, on a day when I needed the love and nurturing of my own mother, she was there to give it.

CHAPTER 4

The Death of a Promise

About three weeks later, I began having pain in my lower right abdomen. It was a sharp pain, and it would take my breath away. I managed to make it through the Memorial Day weekend without much complaint, but I was very aware that something was wrong. I went to work Tuesday morning, and because I felt so poorly, I did not work the entire day. Due to increasing pain, I contacted my doctor on Wednesday morning. I was instructed to come in for an ultrasound, and we made the appointment.

During the ultrasound, the tech asked me more than once to again identify where I was having pain. I told her it was my right side, but she appeared confused. After a few moments of looking around with the ultrasound, she returned with the doctor. After he looked at her findings he asked, "How long have you been hurting on the *left* side?" I corrected him and repeated that it was not on the left but on the *right* side. He insisted that my pain must be on the left side. The tech placed the wand on the left side so the doctor could show me his findings. The problem was indeed on the left side, yet I had no pain there. I was told to get dressed and come to his office to discuss the results. I had no idea what could be wrong, and I was feeling quite alarmed. For a moment, I thought the diagnosis might be something terminal. After all, I had asked God to take my life if I could not conceive. Instead, I discovered something I wasn't expecting at all. The doctor said I needed emergency surgery to remove a tubal pregnancy. I was in disbelief. After all the years of procedures, medications, hope, and heartbreak, I had a non-viable pregnancy. I was speechless.

The nurse brought forms in for me to sign. The procedure would require the removal of one ovary and, if necessary, a complete hysterectomy. I refused to sign the consent. The doctor returned, explaining the depth of danger of waiting until morning for the surgery. He wanted to go to surgery as soon as possible. I would only give permission to remove the left ovary, and if, during the removal something worse should be discovered, they could notify me when I woke up. I would not give blanket consent for the removal of my reproductive organs. I told the doctor that I had a promise from God that I would be a mother, and I could not sign the consent. After several minutes of difficult discussion, he relented and had me sign permission for the lesser surgery. I couldn't help but wonder if this experience was a response to my prayer of ultimatum I had made to God. I returned to the exam room, and Cervadil was placed in my cervix to begin the cervical dilation to hopefully allow a vaginal removal and not an open surgical abdominal access.

I left the doctor's office, returned to my car, and began to cry. I asked the Lord why He was removing every possible avenue, piece by painful piece, of my ever being able to have a baby. Heaven was silent. I sat in the car for a long time before saying, "Though I cannot see the outcome, I cannot see the reason why this is happening; I still believe that all things, according to Romans 8:28, work together for good to them who love the Lord." Even in all the pain and uncertainty, I loved the Lord.

The surgery was able to be done vaginally, so there was no abdominal incision. Physical recovery would be much quicker, and I would return to work in 2 weeks. I did not have a tubal pregnancy, but I had a hydrosalpinx, which is a large amount of fluid in a fallopian tube that can be from infection or severe adhesions, which we knew I had—or Endometriosis, which I also had. It would have likely ruptured, causing further damage.

The summer continued with the emotional roller coaster of still longing for a child. One of the faithful sisters in our church gave me a cassette tape with a sermon called *The Death of a Promise*. The message taught me that sometimes we hold so tightly to something that God cannot work. Because we have devised in our minds what the promise in our life will look like, we forget that God's ways are not our ways. We do not allow for the possibility that God may have other ways of working in our lives. Therefore, we kill the promise before it can transpire.

Our church secretary, Laurie, had been dealing with infertility for about four years. Our pastor's daughter had lost one child, and she also had not been able to conceive for over a year. The three of us leaned on one another during those hard times. It was a bond that couldn't be broken and one that can only be understood if you have faced infertility.

※

One Wednesday in October, as our evening midweek service began, our pastor's daughter went to the altar. In her prayers, I could hear her longing to have a child. I recognized that cry—I had felt it too many times. I knew she was crying out for a baby. The three of us who were facing infertility all began to pray with her. I began to speak to the Lord, recalling how He had promised me almost five years before that I would be a mother. I said in this prayer to Him that I knew somehow, I had missed His promise. I know He is not cruel, and He does what He promises. Nevertheless, I was now thirty-five years old, and I believed it was time to let go of the promise.

I asked God—in the same way that Elijah passed his mantle to Elisha—to allow me to pass my promise to this precious sister, Krista. I had come to love her dearly, and I could not bear the thought of her continuing in her pain. I told the Lord that I would not ask for a child again, but I would be a mother to everyone He put into my life. For the rest of my life, no matter their age, I would be there for those who needed mothering. I told God that I would serve Him faithfully, and my salvation was not predicated on Him giving me what I wanted. I loved and trusted Him, and I understood He knows the things that I don't.

As I finished my prayer, I returned to my seat. I realized two things—an emptiness of sorts and a new peace. It was as though a weight had been lifted. I was going to be okay, and I could accept moving forward without a child if that was what God wanted. I would pray for Krista and Laurie to conceive, and I would stand on my promise as Krista's. I would watch as the Lord answered. I would tell her of my promise, and I told her to expect much affliction, but a pregnancy was sure to come.

When I returned home that evening after service, I told my husband that it was finished. No more pursuing pregnancy. No more consideration of fostering—it was over. I explained what had happened, and he asked if I could live with that decision. I confidently, though painfully, said yes, I could and would.

I went to work the next morning and shared all that had transpired with my co-worker. This woman had endured infertility as well, and she was an ear I knew would understand my decision. I was making my new resolve public—this was the end of the road.

CHAPTER 5

The Promise Fulfilled

The following Sunday morning, a trusted friend and sister in the Lord came to me at church with obvious angst. When I asked her what was wrong, she told me she had a Word from God for me. She was hesitant to tell me, but I insisted that she share. I assured her that I trusted her walk with God, and if she had a Word from God, I believed it was true. She told me that the Lord had spoken to her to tell me to accept whatever it was that he had for me. Believing she was speaking about the events in recent days, I told her that I already had accepted God's will and was at peace with it.

On Sunday evening, I decided I would stand at the sanctuary doors and greet others as they came in. I had never done it before, and as I was greeting people, a young woman and her baby came in. I asked who she was with, and she said it was only her and her child. I invited them to sit with me, but she declined and asked where the youth group usually sits. I directed her and watched her walk to that area and take a seat. As the music began to play, I took my seat. I looked over at the young woman who was standing with the music and noticed she was crying. I silently prayed for her, and as I did so, I felt the Lord speak to me. I began to earnestly pray—whatever the need in her life, the Lord would meet it. I felt as though God wanted me to go pray for her directly, and while I hesitated, two women in the church laid hands on the young woman to pray for her too. The young woman was weeping, and again, the Lord pressed upon me that the woman needed my prayers.

I immediately went to her. She opened her eyes, and I asked if I could hand her baby to my mother while I prayed for her. As soon as I handed her baby to my mom, the young woman took my hands and pulled me to the front altar of the church. I began praying with her. I was praying out loud and spoke two specific prayers over her—prayers I had never spoken over anyone. They were prayers about the woman's life, and it was as though God was showing me details about the young mother's trials. She opened her eyes and asked me how I knew the things I was praying. I told her that I only knew her name, but God knows everything about you and is reaching for you tonight. The young woman prayed and poured her heart out to the Lord for several minutes before the service transitioned to the sermon. I asked her not to leave until I had a chance to speak to her, and she agreed. Meanwhile, she left her baby with my mom.

After the service, I invited her into one of the church offices and asked her who she came to church with. I also asked her if there were any needs in her life I could help her pray for. She stopped my questions and told me there was something she needed to tell me. To my surprise, she told me that God had spoken to her about me three times throughout the evening. The young woman began to explain that, while she had one baby I had met, she was also pregnant with another child. She explained that the baby's father was no longer in her life, and she did not feel she was ready to raise another baby on her own. In her desperation, she had recently been asking God who she could give the child to—who would love and care for it. The Lord led her to my church.

She told me that upon entering our church that evening, God assured her that I was the one He had prepared for her child. After she was seated, she began to pray, telling the Lord that if I was the one, I should come and pray for her. When I approached her and asked to pray with her, she thought it must be me. When I had begun to speak to her around the altar about the things in her life that God had shown me, she felt God impress upon her that it was confirmed—I was the one.

She then looked at me and said, "May I ask you something?" I told her that she could.

She asked, "You don't have any children, do you?"

I responded with, "No, as a matter of fact, I do not."

The young woman then said, "I know you must think I am completely crazy, but I am telling you this is your baby. If you have a lawyer, I will sign papers so you will know I am serious."

I was in shock. Just four days ago, I gave my promise away. Now, I was overwhelmed and in a measure of disbelief. I asked how far along she was, and she said she guessed about six months or so. She shared that she had not had any prenatal care up to that point and did not yet have a due date.

After gathering my thoughts, I told her that because I am a nurse, I realize how critical it is that she be seen to make sure both she and the baby are healthy. I told her I would pay for her first visit, and that I could arrange an appointment with my doctor if she would like. She agreed. I asked for her phone number and address, and she willingly gave them to me. I pleaded with her to listen to me very carefully—if she was not completely honest with me and if there was any chance that she would change her mind, I begged her not to bring this to me anymore. I shared with her that I had been on a very long and painful journey to become a mother, and if I had even one more disappointment, I would surely die. I would still pay for her first visit to the doctor, but I begged her not to mislead me. She assured me that I was the mother of her unborn child. I told her I would make an appointment for prenatal care in the morning and call her with an appointment time. She agreed. We hugged, retrieved her baby from my mother, and said goodnight.

I brought my mother and Jim into the office, and I shared with them the conversation. I was in shock and disbelief; they were crying and laughing with joy while I was sobbing with fear. Could this be real? Was this God's plan? What about giving away my promise?

When I arrived home, I shared everything that had happened with my husband. We both sat, trying to make sense of everything. I decided to call my doctor even though it was late on Sunday night. He returned my call and was overjoyed. He said to call the office in the morning and tell them to schedule her for that afternoon.

I made the appointment for Wednesday. The initial appointment was good, and an ultrasound was scheduled for the following week. I took the young pregnant mother and her child out for lunch and back to their home with a promise to provide transport to the next appointment and offered to supply any needs for her and the baby.

The following week, we returned for the ultrasound. I will never forget that day. We were given a due date of February 2—my grandmother's birthday. We learned that the baby was a boy, and while watching the movements on the screen, he did a flip and turned his head toward us. He moved his arm slowly with his hands wide open as if waving, and he brought his thumb up to his mouth. I will hold that memory in my mind forever.

During that time, I was cautiously optimistic, fearing that something could still go wrong. But as the days passed, I began to believe that this was indeed my time. It was glorious. I began making all the necessary preparations to begin caring for the baby that was to come.

The ladies of the church celebrated with me by having a Noah's Ark themed baby shower with 63 people in attendance. I felt loved and was showered with so much support and many gifts. It was incredible. My sister's twins, now ten years old, were at the shower. There were so many gifts given to us at the shower that we required two cars to pack it all. We took everything home to our nursery. Taylor rode with me in my car, and on the way home, he asked me if I would still love him once baby Noah arrived. I assured him that he and his brother were my first babies forever, and they would never be replaced.

I continued to transport the mother and child to all appointments and provided groceries in the house throughout the pregnancy. Then, on January 31, at a routine appointment, it was discovered that she had preeclampsia and would need to be induced for the safety of both her and the baby. We drove from the office to the hospital and had some friends from the church meet us there to take care of her toddler. The young pregnant mother was admitted and received her IV Pitocin to start labor at 1:30 pm. I would be in the labor room with her and would be her support person.

I called my mother, the church, and my closest friends. My husband had been at a dental appointment at the same time and was having oral surgery, so we decided it best for him to go home and sleep a while before coming to the hospital. The hospital waiting room was soon filled with those who were there to support us and await the arrival of baby Noah.

There was a new woman who had been attending our church and had known the young mother a few years prior. She also came to the hospital during labor. When asked if I minded if she were to come in as her support person during labor, I agreed immediately.

As the contractions became more frequent and increased in intensity, we three ladies offered her support. Mom and I were on each side of her while her friend was at the top of her head. Once she reached 10 cm dilated, the doctor came in, and soon after, a baby was born. The few seconds it took for him to take his first breath seemed like an eternity. Then, the sound I had been longing to hear for years overtook the silent room—he began to cry! That cry was from heaven, and it was a promise fulfilled. God answered every prayer and wiped away all my tears in that moment. At 1:17 am on February 1, Noah James Henderson, 7lbs, 12oz, light hair and eyes, perfect in every way, was here. They handed him to me, wrapped in a blanket. I looked at his little face, his eyes wide open as we looked at each other for the first time. I said, "What took you so long? I have been waiting for you my whole life."

My husband had arrived and was waiting outside. He was in the hallway with five ladies from the church who were my dear friends. They reported back to me that once they said the baby was coming, they heard the final push and then the silence until he cried. They said they heard me let out a cry, and there was not a dry eye in the hallway. The prayers that had been prayed for so many years were now being realized.

My husband was in excruciating pain from his procedure, so I insisted he go home. My mother said her goodbyes and allowed myself, the baby boy, and this brave young woman to be alone. Once they left, I was still holding baby Noah. I asked her if she wanted to hold or see him, and she said yes. I brought him to her. She held him close to her and said, "He doesn't look like me, does he?" Then she said these words:

"Come, take your baby."

Her bravery and her willingness to be used as an instrument of God left me astounded by her maturity at only twenty years old.

Following adoption procedures, the hospital staff soon came in to take the young woman into another room. Once she was taken away, I was told by the nursing staff that there were no other babies in the nursery and no other mothers in labor. Because it was so quiet, I could come into the newborn nursery and assist with his bath and checks if I would like. What a blessing and honor that was. Later, I was escorted to a courtesy room and told to get into a hospital gown and bed, like all new mothers.

Words fail me to express what it was like to lay that precious baby boy on my chest and have him begin to root for my breast! My colostrum had come in only hours before, just in time. God is an on-time God!

I was given a supplemental nurser that went around my neck on a string, like a necklace. The supplemental nurser is a flat-sided bottle on both sides that we put formula in as it was likely that I may not produce enough milk to completely sustain the nutritional needs of the baby. He latched on rather easily, and I felt him bond with me physically and emotionally. It was one of the most beautiful experiences of my life. Our pediatrician came to congratulate me and give me one piece of advice: "What you do once, you do forever. The habits you make in childcare will be formed early and likely stay with you, so make good choices now." I still live by what he said all these years later.

☙

We were able to leave the hospital when Noah was 17 hours old. Once we entered the house and locked the door behind us, it became real. We were home. This was not a dream. It was real. I could breathe.

For years, I had dreamed of becoming a parent, only to wake up from that dream heartbroken. I would often cry myself back to sleep, feeling the weight of my empty arms. Because of those dreams, I was afraid to go to sleep.

I had an irrational fear that if I closed my eyes and went to sleep, I would awaken to find that Noah had been a dream and did not exist. For the first six weeks of his life, I slept in the living room with him in my arms. I finally conceded to having the bassinet up against the bed and always slept with one hand on the baby. I would leave the shower door open while showering, refusing to close my eyes even under the running water for fear I would open my eyes and he would be gone. It took about six months for those fears to leave.

When Noah was five weeks old, on March 8, 2001, we went to the courthouse to finalize his adoption. This was the day that I could say with no reservations—I was indeed Noah's Mother.

I had been standing on the promises of Psalm 37:4 for many years. On that day, the Lord proved His Word. He gave me the desires of my heart.

> *Let every thing that hath breath praise the Lord. Praise ye the Lord.* — Psalm 150:6

I could never praise Him enough for ending the pain of infertility and giving me joy unspeakable and full of glory.

CHAPTER 6

New Beginnings

While preparing for Noah's birth, Krista had found out that she was pregnant! How wonderful is our God? Laurie came to me in December to tell me that she had been to the doctor and found out she was also pregnant. Glory to God in the highest! We were rejoicing together because our God had proven Himself so many times. What a miraculous answer to our prayer.

Just as God had spoken to me, Krista's promise came with much pain. Her pregnancy was difficult, but today, baby Samuel is with us—a testimony to the goodness of God.

On July 31, 2001, Laurie's baby girl, Derah, was born. Then, with Samuel being born the next day, exactly six months to the day after Noah, the promise I had passed to Krista was delivered just as our Lord had promised. By the end of that year, all of the women who had been praying for children received the answers they had been praying for.

During the pregnancy of Laurie and Krista, the same sister who had given me the cassette tape *Death of A Promise* said, "Look around—there is no other baby in our church right now. You have the only infant. That is unusual for a church of our size. The Lord is giving you this season and allowing all to see His might through you."

I have kept those words in my heart all these years.

☙

After Noah's birth, it was time for me to consider the warnings my doctor had given me about my future health. I never had the surgery that he insisted upon, and it was starting to catch up with me. After giving it much thought, we decided it was best for me to have surgery and remove any possibilities of ailments that would endanger my life. I went into the hospital confident and at peace. My prayers had been answered, and I could move forward without the pain of PCOS and Endometriosis that had plagued me for so many years. The surgery went well. I was in the hospital for three days, which also marked the first time I had ever been away from Noah since his birth.

During that time, my husband and I experienced many trials reminiscent of the lowest points in our marriage. My husband had offered much help and support throughout our struggles with infertility. Nevertheless, my relationship with the church had often been a source of conflict between us that grew into larger issues. Sadly, we soon divorced and were forced to split our time with baby Noah.

Noah spent time with his father, and those days were difficult for me. I would have never believed that after all we had gone through, our marriage would come to an end, but I was determined that Noah would be allowed to love his dad in my home. I did not want our new son to be used as a tool in divorce. Noah was growing every day. I had to find other ways to fill my time when he was not at home and trust the Lord to watch him. Childhood goes by so quickly. I heard someone say that while parenting young children, the days are so long, but the years are so short. It is a hard truth that I have passed on to young mothers in my life.

I was a Licensed Practical Nurse, and God made the way for me to return to school to become a Registered Nurse—my other lifelong dream. Once again, God proved Himself faithful in giving me the desires of my heart. He is Jehovah Jireh—my provider. I trust that He has all my tomorrows in His control, just as He had control of all my yesterdays.

> *When thou liest down, thou shalt not be afraid: yea, thou shalt lie down, and thy sleep shall be sweet.* — Proverbs 3:24

During that time, my mother and I decided to buy a home together. My stepfather was ill, and I was a single mother with a job, going to school full-time. My mother spent time with my son, and Noah was as happy and as loved as any child could ever be.

I began to date a man from our church—a man I had actually met while in nursing school 12 years earlier. Chuck was over the computer lab at my community college during my pursuit of becoming a Licensed Practical Nurse. I don't think I would have graduated if he had not been in the computer lab—essentially teaching me from scratch how to make documents and complete assignments. I was completely computer illiterate. Chuck was kind and helpful. He became my lifeline in the lab.

Ironically, a couple of years later, I came into work one day in a retirement community health center to see Chuck in the hallway crying because his precious grandmother had been hit by a car while crossing the street; she was now in our care for a broken pelvis. Due to the reaction of the pain medications, she wasn't being very kind to this man who adored her! We assured him it was the medication. She really did not mean those words, and we would take good care of her. She would be back to her normal, kind self soon enough. That was indeed the case.

A year or so later, this same man was sitting in my church one Sunday morning as a guest with one of our members. It was nice to see him again, and he assured me his grandmother was well. Soon, he became a born-again Christian and made our church his home. Chuck was very interested in helping my stepfather, who was deaf, to understand the preached word. Because my stepfather's primary language was American Sign Language, he had difficulty understanding the preacher without interpretation. My mother was his interpreter but was not able to go to men's meetings. Chuck became a diligent student of sign language. Within one year he was teaching my mother's advanced ASL class weekly. He became a very close friend of my parents. We would all go out to dinner most Sunday evenings after church. As fate would have it, Chuck and I fell in love.

My brother was retiring from the United States Navy after having served for more than 20 years, and we were flying out to Washington State to attend his retirement festivities. I recall this night vividly. We both realized something was happening between us. We had gone to Wednesday evening service. My sister, her husband, and the twins were to meet at my house after, around 9 pm, to stay the night and be ready for the ride to the airport at 3 am. I had made a pot of soup prior to going to church. Chuck asked if we could go out to dinner. I said we could not, as my family was likely already at my house, and I had food prepared. I invited him to join us, and he accepted.

After everyone finished eating, I was scurrying around doing last-minute things before leaving town for a week. One by one, the kids and then the adults dropped off to sleep, knowing they could only sleep for a few hours. Chuck followed me from room to room as I busied about doing all the last-minute checks. Finally, I stopped and looked at him, asking if there was something he needed. I really needed him to leave so I could shower. I no longer had any time left to even nap. Chuck responded with a yes, saying there was something he would like to speak with me about. I suggested we step outside so as not to awaken anyone, as there were sleepers on couches and in beds. I also thought this would get him on his way out the door!

I cannot explain what happened as we walked out the front door of my home. It was as if a blinder had been removed. All of a sudden, I looked at him and a surge of feelings overtook me. Chuck took me by the shoulders and said these words: "I don't know what is happening here, but something IS happening. Promise me you will come back home." I stood there stunned, as, unknown to ANYONE but Jesus during my prayer time, I had every intention of moving to Washington!

I wanted to escape the pain of divorce, I wanted to travel as a nurse, and I wanted to do something I had never done before. I had a resume in hand and had been online looking at jobs available to nurses in the Bremerton, Washington area. But, when I looked into his eyes and saw something I had never seen before, without thinking, I said, "Yes, I promise." He hugged me and drove away. I stood there for a few moments and then ran inside, awakened my mother and sister, telling them what had just transpired. They both responded that it was about time the two of us saw we were meant to be together. Everyone else had seen it for quite some time! Our blinders had been removed—this began our love story.

As soon as we returned from Rick's beautiful week of celebration of his service to our wonderful country, Chuck and I began hours and hours of talking on the phone late into the night and emailing one another during the daytime hours. I was walking on a cloud.

Chuck and I began making wedding plans in the coming fall. We agreed that we were determined to allow our home to always be a home of refuge.

One night, while we were walking on the campus of Indiana University we went into Beck Chapel, a lovely little chapel on campus, quaint and beautiful. Chuck knelt at my feet and began praying blessings over me. We vowed to the Lord that night to always allow our home to be a place of healing, a place of ministry, a refuge for the hurting. Obviously, we thought that meant that we would open our home for meals, bible study, fellowship, teaching, anything to help the hurting. BUT OH, did our Lord have another plan.

About two weeks before we married, one of the ladies in our church came to us and said she had a dream about us the night before. She dreamed we would have a baby girl! The week prior, Chuck, while in prayer, had a vision. For a few moments, he could clearly see a wrapped pink bundle being handed down to him from the Heavens. He shared that with me, and we discussed the fact that I cannot have children. He said no matter, obviously, somehow or someway, the Lord would be bringing a pink bundle into our lives. Of course, after the dream was shared with us, we knew that God was preparing us for a bigger plan—His plan.

I was finishing my Registered Nurse clinical the week before our wedding, and on Wednesday, I was on a clinical site. At 7:30 am, before starting my clinical, I picked up the local newspaper to see the headline of a terrible case of abuse. As I read the article, I discovered that the victims of the abuse were Noah's biological mother and sibling. Initially, I thought to myself how thankful I was knowing that Noah wasn't subjected to that abuse. Next, I wondered what the poor mother and child were going to do. The article said the children were removed by the authorities, and my heart and mind began to race.

What could we do to help them? I immediately contacted Chuck as he was just arriving at his office. I told him to look at the paper. I asked what we were going to do.

His response? "Let's go get them."

I replied, "We are getting married in two days."

He said, "Good, they will have a two-parent home."

I rebutted, "But our house isn't big enough!"

His answer? "We will buy a bigger house."

Although I was hesitant at the idea, wondering if we had enough space, Chuck assured me that we would get a bigger house if need be. These children needed a home.

November 17, 2006: We were married in a lovely, intimate ceremony by our pastor in Beck Chapel. The twins, now

NEW BEGINNINGS

16 years old, had been in our wedding, along with Noah, who was now 5 years old. Our wedding colors were pink and black. On the way to the tuxedo fittings two weeks before the wedding, Noah had declared that he would not be wearing pink because he would be wearing a red tuxedo. We discussed that the color was pink and not red and that Mommy would help him choose something pink. Noah was adamant that red was the color. I called Chuck, thinking he would have a united front with me regarding the wedding colors. He responded that this was Noah's wedding too, and just as we had chosen what we were to wear on our special day, he should be allowed and encouraged to do the same. Noah looked breathtakingly beautiful on our wedding day in a red shirt, red bow tie, and red cummerbund with his black tuxedo. Chuck was wise in that decision.

We enjoyed a lovely reception with our close family and friends, then a quick getaway as I had to return for nursing finals the following Monday. It was a three-day work/school week, as it was the week of Thanksgiving. After celebrating the holiday and returning to school, we contacted the local Department of Child Services to see how we could help the children, Noah's half-siblings, the ones from the newspaper article. I spoke to the investigator and caseworker who had removed the children. I told them who I was and that we had a biological half-sibling of the abused children. I assured them that we would be willing to do anything to help the situation. The caseworker said it was all confidential information, and she could not verify that they were in the care of her department. Nevertheless, I told her we were willing to give them a safe place while the case was unfolding and that I would continue to contact her for placement of the children until the situation was resolved.

After receiving no response, Chuck and I decided to go down to the office in person. We met with the foster care specialist, and, to our surprise, none of our messages had been received by the office to that point. Still, we began the long and expensive process of doing all that we could to make sure that the children would be placed in our home.

One night, after returning home from church, Chuck and I had a difficult decision to make. Should we continue to have the children removed from their present foster situation or allow things to play out as they would? We knew in our hearts that the children were not in a healthy home. Over time, that fact became more evident. Unfortunately, there was nothing we could do about the situation at the time. With heavy hearts, we went to prayer and released the children into the arms of the Lord. We decided we would withdraw our petition to adopt them. We prayed for them and their biological mother every night. We also shared with Noah that they would not be coming to live with us. While sad, Noah was accepting, and we prepared to move on.

Just as I had once ached over my inability to conceive, I began to ache for the adoption of those children. Much like the story of Noah, the way I wanted things to turn out was different than God's plans for me. Chuck shared with me that he felt we would adopt a baby girl soon. In time, his thoughts proved to be true.

CHAPTER 7

The Vision Becomes a Reality

In May of 2009, while cleaning our bathroom, I had a fleeting thought that today was the day a baby girl was coming. Within moments, the phone rang. It was the Department of Child Services asking if we would consider placement of a child! During the struggle for Noah's siblings, we had become a certified foster home. The person from Child Services told me that there was a baby girl who had suffered severe abuse and needed a home. Would we take her? I was a nurse, and she needed a medically safe home, so they decided to contact us and request placement. Without hesitation, I said yes. She was in Riley Children's Hospital and would be released in two days. I immediately called Chuck at work, realizing I had said yes to placement without consulting him. When I told him the situation, he responded, "You said yes, didn't you?" He never ceases to amaze me with his depth of compassion.

On Wednesday, two days later, we were on our way to the hospital when we received a call that the baby was in dire condition. She was having seizures and would most likely not survive due to her trauma. We were devastated. Chuck and I pulled over on the side of the road and began to pray for this baby girl, who, through no fault of her own, was injured by the ones who were supposed to protect her. She was fighting for her life at only nine weeks old. We returned home, heavy-hearted and concerned for the life we had not even met, yet already loved.

The next morning, May 21, we received a phone call from the social worker at Riley Hospital saying that they had no explanation as to why, but the baby girl was much better and was well enough to be released that day! They asked if we could pick her up, and we said yes. I called Chuck with the news, and he left work to get me and head to the hospital. While waiting for Chuck, I made arrangements for my mother to get Noah. I was nervous but so excited to meet this baby girl.

When we arrived at the hospital, the social worker took us up to the unit. We were met by nursing staff who began discharge, teaching us the very specific needs of the infant. She was underweight, had suffered head trauma due to shaken baby syndrome, she was blind in her left eye, having multiple seizures, and had some potential swallowing issues. It was a frightening undertaking, but it was one we were willing to accept. After an hour or so of teaching, we asked the nurse if we could see her. She was surprised

THE VISION BECOMES A REALITY

that we had not first met the baby. We explained that we had not even seen a photo of her yet.

We were taken to the room. Her name was Lilly; she was on her tummy as she looked up at me. We locked eyes—it was as if we both knew this was a moment that would forever change our lives. If ever there is love at first sight, that was it. She was a tiny baby with a turban bandage on her head, an arm board with an IV in her left arm, and an O2 sensor on her right foot. She was so delicate and fragile. My heart could not take knowing why she was in that situation. The doctor came in as I asked if I could hold her. She was wonderfully kind and helped get me into the rocking chair. She placed the baby in my arms, attachments and all. When Lilly was placed into my arms, I felt the exact rush of emotion that I had felt the first time I held Noah. She was forever emblazoned in my heart.

Lilly was not quite 10lbs, uncommon for her age. We were told more about her injuries that day. Lilly had been life-lined to Riley Children's Hospital in grave condition. Upon arrival, she was immediately taken into surgery, and in surgery the blood was aspirated and sent to the lab. The lab discovered three levels of blood, indicating that Lilly had been abused more than once. My mind could barely comprehend the information. We also discovered that Lilly's parents had given her a pacifier—a pacifier that they insisted should be shared with the dog. This also created health problems for the child. Injuries on Lilly's cheek indicated the dog had likely taken the pacifier from her at some point. She still has a scar from the incident. My heart melted for her, but I knew the Lord had brought her to us. No matter what, she would be forever loved by us.

We had to bring Lilly back to the hospital the following day for further evaluation. In any case of suspected abuse with injury to a child, the child is given a complete body x-ray. Every bone in the body is imaged to look for a current or healing fracture. This process took forty-five minutes, and we had to stop periodically due to Lilly's seizures. No broken bones were noted, but the process had to be repeated two weeks later to rule out fractures or evidence of healing that could have been missed on the first set of images.

Many doctor visits were scheduled as baby Lilly required much care. Suffering extensive injuries, Lilly was on a long road to recovery. Her biological parents were allowed to visit with her three times per week—a taxing schedule given the number of doctors' appointments we were maintaining at the time. Chuck and I worked hard to be certain that everything was done in the baby's best interest. We were fortunate to have an amazing court-appointed advocate and case worker who worked tirelessly for Lilly's best interest and tried to help the young couple as well. Lilly's medical needs continued to be complex. She was showing signs of silent aspiration, and I urged that she be given a comprehensive swallow study to check. The study concluded she was aspirating, causing respiratory infections. As if all of that weren't challenging enough, Lilly could only be fed by a tube until she was four years old.

Lilly was also blind in one eye. At her first eye appointment, we were shown retinal scans. There were so many hemorrhages in both eyes—caused by the force of the shaking she suffered and possibly blunt force trauma. Realizing all that Lilly had endured was a paralyzing moment for me. The doctors told us to patch the right eye daily. By covering her good eye, and with proper treatment, her bad eye could be induced to see once again. Lilly could not tolerate loud noises, so we kept the television and radio off while at home. I would sit in the rocking chair with her, reading out loud, praying, and singing to her.

During Lilly's first year of life, we were told that she would likely never be able to go to public school. Due to the severity of her injuries and the damage to the frontal lobe of her brain, it was believed that she would not be able to grasp concepts such as sentence structure or math. She would likely never walk without braces or be able to jump or run. Still, I refused to accept the report. God is a healer, and He is faithful. How many miracles in the New Testament were performed for the sake of children? I know He answers prayer, and I continued to pray over her and continued to pray for healing.

Lilly was diagnosed with Cerebral Palsy. Her calf muscles were extremely tight, hindering her from walking and running. When Lilly began to take steps, she was more unbalanced than usual and was fitted for braces to hold her feet and ankles firmly.

Despite all her troubles, Lilly was a determined child. When we would take the braces off at night, she would walk around furniture and grab anything she could hold onto. At age two, after much therapy, it was decided she would not need braces any longer. She was now a "tiptoe" walker, but she was also a tiptoe runner! She was fast and safe on her feet. Goodbye, braces!

Blood draws were often the most challenging medical procedures Lilly had to endure. They became so frequent that Lilly was fearful of doctors who approached us, worried that needle pricks were coming next.

The other traumatic recurring event for Lilly was EEG. This is a measure of brain activity and is best done while the child is sleeping. EEGs would be scheduled first thing in the morning, usually at 8 am. Lilly would need to be kept awake from midnight until the time of the test to ensure she would go to sleep. It was awful for her, and it was awful for us. Keeping her awake, sitting in the bathtub with her, walking around, playing outside—anything on earth to keep her and us awake. At the hospital, she would have metal electrodes placed on her head, completely painless. She would have multiple wires attached and then would go to sleep in my arms while they ran the test.

When Lilly was four years old, she had been seizure-free for two years. She had also been off of all medications for a year, so we scheduled her final EEG.

THE VISION BECOMES A REALITY

When her neurologist called us with the results, there was no evidence of any abnormal brain activity in Lilly! Furthermore, after four years of physical therapy, occupational therapy, braces, and Botox injections into her calves, Lilly was discharged from all care! Her Cerebral Palsy diagnosis was also removed—Lilly was physically healed! When the neurologist marveled, we told her that it was not us but the power of our God who had healed Lilly. The neurologist responded, "You almost caused me to believe."

When Lilly was six months old, as was my routine, I would lay her on my bed and choose a patch for her eye. One morning, I patched her good eye, then moved to the right to pick up something from the dresser. I noticed Lilly turned her head to follow me. Could that be right? Then I moved to the left. She turned her head to the left in my direction. I moved several times without speaking, as I did not want her to be able to follow my voice. Suddenly, I realized that she must be seeing my movements! I called the Riley Eye Clinic, and they made an appointment to see her the following day. After the appointment it was confirmed—Lilly could see! What a victory! Lilly's eyesight was responding. I thanked God and prayed every day that He would restore her vision through the process, and He did just that. Once Lilly began pulling the patches off, we had to use eye drops to dilate the eye and allow the weaker eye to work harder. By the time Lilly was seven years old, we were told that her brain had recovered all that it would and that it was likely that Lilly would even be able to drive one day. She would wear glasses the rest of her life—but she could see!

Because Lilly's biological parents' relationship had deteriorated, they could not demonstrate their capacity to care for the child. After fifteen months of foster care, the Department of Child Services allowed us to move forward with adoption. On February 13, 2011, we were to have an all-day trial to hear the case for termination of parental rights. The biological father asked my husband if he could speak to him before going into the courtroom. Lilly's mother and father had decided that they did not want courtroom proceedings to progress, and they had decided not to contest our adoption of Lilly. The next day, Lilly had her final visit with her biological parents. During that visit, she had a seizure—but it was the last seizure Lilly ever had.

The judge set a final date for adoption. It was March 8, 2011, exactly ten years to the day since Noah's adoption. During the adoption hearing, we decided that we would change the baby's name. This child who had endured so much had been blessed with a new beginning. We felt that new beginnings deserved a new name. It was on that day that we decided to give her the name Lilly DeAnna Aikman, after my sister Deede. (We now call them Big Dee and Little Dee.) Much of my family was present in the courtroom that day to witness another miracle God had performed in my life.

THE VISION BECOMES A REALITY

God has completely healed Lilly, and she is a miracle of biblical proportions. Lilly is an excellent vocalist. She sings on the praise team at our church and in competitions. She is one of the quickest runners on the school track team, and she has even taken ballet lessons. In short, Lilly has zero evidence of a traumatic brain injury. She is completely restored.

March 8 is a holiday looked forward to every year in our home. We celebrate each child, and they receive a gift as we tell them their story. Adoption is a celebrated word in our home.

When Noah was ten, and Lilly was two, I decided that I wanted to continue to help children in need. I became a Court Appointed Special Advocate (CASA) myself. I took the training and performed those duties for the next two years while also considering fostering more children.

CHAPTER 8

The Arrival of Nathan

In February 2013, I was invited to be part of a ladies' Bible study that was reading the book *Radical* by David Platt. The book caused me to take a hard look at whether I was following God or was I chasing material dreams. I began to reconsider passions and callings throughout my life that had, perhaps, been left behind. Whose kingdom was I building? Mine? Or the Lord's?

I was in the laundry room one afternoon while my husband was painting our daughter's room when the song *Kings and Queens* by Audio Adrenaline came on the radio. The words of the song began to penetrate my thoughts, heart, and soul. How could I look away from the need? I knew there were many children out there who needed a loving home. As the song says...

"Open our hearts and our doors to love the least of these. If not us, who will be like Jesus to the least of these?"

The words struck me like a chord, and I began to cry. I walked to the door of my daughter's room, where Chuck was on the ladder. Without turning around, he said, "We aren't done, are we?" No, we weren't.

The following week, I told the CASA office that I would be resigning as a volunteer and opening up my home for children. They were nothing but supportive. We contacted the Department of Child Services to reinstate our license. By June of 2013, we were ready to foster.

On July 15, 2013, we headed to church camp with our children, camper in tow. As we got closer to the campgrounds, my phone began to ring. It was the Department of Child Services—there was a six-month-old baby boy in need. I asked how soon the baby needed to be picked up, and they said within the hour. I contacted my husband, and we discussed the situation, eventually deciding to accept placement. Chuck would pick up the baby, and the two would come up to church camp later in the evening.

It was incredibly hot that July day as we headed to the campgrounds. After accepting placement, the children and I discussed the new baby boy coming to our home and the care he would need. Suddenly, as I was unloading the car, the kids came to me and said they wanted to go home. They told me that the baby would need to see his new home, not the camper. Furthermore, they were excited to

THE ARRIVAL OF NATHAN

meet the baby and thought we should leave. Knowing that it would mean missing church camp, the children wanted to be a part of welcoming the new baby into our lives. What wisdom, out of the mouths of babes indeed. We repacked the car and headed home.

As we pulled into the driveway, we could see that Chuck had just pulled in and parked his car. We all ran to meet baby Nathan. When my husband lifted that tiny boy with the biggest brown eyes I had ever seen out of the car seat and handed him to me, I was smitten! What a beautiful baby boy. Nathan looked at me, reached for me, laid his head on my chest, and went right to sleep. He was precious indeed. Nathan spent most of the next three days and nights asleep. When he awakened, he was a sweet, smiley, happy child. We were all in love with him.

Much like Lilly, Nathan had parents who were unsuited to care for him, and the Department of Child Services soon released him for adoption. On August 20, 2015, Nathan became our third adopted child. Lilly was his "little Momma," and Noah was his favorite buddy.

CHAPTER 9

Conversations with the Lord

We didn't adopt all the children we fostered. One set of siblings we cared for over the course of nearly a year were ultimately reunified with their parents. We remain in contact with them to this day, and we are thankful for the role we played in their lives.

We also never stopped praying for Noah's three biological siblings who we tried to take in years before. Through social media, I discovered that all three had been adopted. I also stayed in contact with Noah's biological mother—the woman who listened to the voice of God and started me on the journey to becoming a mother.

When I first became a CASA in 2011, I had a conversation with one of the workers who was familiar with the case of Noah's siblings. I asked if she remembered me—the woman who had tried so hard to place the children in her home. The caseworker said she didn't, but she wished she had known me at the time. I didn't understand what she meant by this at first, but it became clear some years later.

☙

In April of 2017, we received a call that Lexi, one of Noah's half-siblings, was in need. She had been out of the adoptive home she was placed in for a long period and was now in a residential facility. They asked if we would be willing to be a part of her team. Of course, we said yes! We agreed to meet Lexi and her caseworker for lunch. She was fourteen years old, but we had not seen her since she was six. We met at a restaurant, and it was clear that Lexi was feeling very anxious. We offered for the caseworker to come to our home if it would help Lexi feel more at ease. Lexi walked through our house and made herself at home, marking the beginning of an answered prayer we had long awaited.

The next day, Lexi had a hearing. The judge said Lexi must be moved from the facility, and our name was mentioned as a placement option for the child. The judge said if we would accept her, it would be with his blessing. We received the phone call that afternoon. We accepted, and the next day she moved in. Finally, our lost daughter was coming home! That was on Good Friday. She was moving in just before her birthday, which was the day after Easter. There would be much celebrating indeed.

In our home, we prioritized a Christian culture of modesty. For children who have not been taught the value of a modest life, much less been raised in a Christian environment, this can be challenging. Nevertheless, Lexi responded well to the challenge and eventually began to thrive. She began attending the private Christian school our children went to and was quickly making friends.

Because of the abuse she suffered in the past, it was, at times, difficult to keep a positive relationship with Lexi. We were able to adopt her after nearly two years, but Lexi initially resisted the idea. It took time for trust and care to be sown into our relationship with her—a lesson that all parents who adopt children will eventually learn.

Lexi is a bright young woman with goals for her future. There were many challenging days, but with love, patience, prayer, and a close community of family and friends, Lexi blossomed. Lexi graduated high school and was accepted into college. At seventeen, Lexi moved two hours away into student housing and began living as a young adult. Today, she is pursuing a career in law enforcement and is an active member of the Army National Guard. Lexi has strong survival instincts and will certainly use her pain to help others overcome. We love her and have a positive relationship with her today.

Much like Lexi, Noah's other half-siblings were suffering abuse and were in need of placement. In January of 2018, we took in the youngest of the siblings. Known by her previous family as Maddie, she wanted to return to her birth-name of Kayla after removal from the home. While with us for a time, Kayla was eventually placed in a treatment facility where she could begin to heal. We love Kayla and pray that she will find a place of healing and restoration. We hope to always be available to her. God is still writing her story, and I know that one day, all of the things she has endured that were meant for her destruction will be used by God for good to her.

☙

2019 brought Jazzy to us. She was diagnosed with Leukemia and was hospitalized when we first met her. We were told there would be multiple trips to the clinic two hours away and several overnight stays. We discussed it as a family and decided that if the Lord wished us to take the journey with this child, then we would be willing. We made arrangements to meet Jazzy and her medical team on a Thursday. When we arrived, we spent some time talking with the medical staff about Leukemia, her treatment, and what we could expect. We were given a large binder full of information. It was overwhelming, and we were questioning our decision—but we felt God's presence and His peace. He assured us that we were in His will. We were also given a list of questions that Jazzy had prepared to meet us!

Jazzy's questions went something like this: Did we have other kids? Did we have pets? Were we nice? Did we go to church? She was a sweet little six-year-old girl. I won't forget walking into the hospital room to see her with very little hair remaining that was obviously once very long. She had a small cluster on each side of the top of her head—all other strands were just wisps and reminders of what used to be. I instantly felt a protectiveness well up inside of me.

> *Bless the Lord, O my soul: and all that is within me, bless his holy name. Bless the Lord, O my soul, and forget not all his benefits: Who forgiveth all thine iniquities; who healeth all thy diseases; — Psalm 103:1-3*

Jazzy had an IV attached to a port in her chest. She pulled around an IV pole that she had named "Stan." Jazzy was alone in her room but appeared very confident and comfortable. She had piles of drawings and legos, a dresser-top full of snacks, and the TV playing a favorite movie. Jazzy allowed us to sit and talk with her while we got to know one another. We told her we had seen her list of questions and would be happy to answer them for her. Jazzy was articulate and sweet; we were instantly smitten. We spent about an hour with her and then spoke again with her medical team, who believed she would be ready for release from the hospital in four days. She had been there for more than two months. While her mother's boyfriend had taken care of her to the best of his ability, neglect had characterized Jazzy's care up to that point.

In the weeks leading up to her being placed in the hospital, Jazzy's mother had an argument with Jazzy's legal guardian and decided to sign her out of school one day and take her to live in a pop-up camper out of state.

One evening, some people came to the camper to "party." A woman at the party noticed Jazzy's frail condition and urged the biological mother to take Jazzy to the hospital. Jazzy's mother was unaware and unconcerned with her condition, as she was not her normal caregiver. Nevertheless, after much urging, the mother took Jazzy to a walk-in clinic. They quickly realized how grave her condition was, and Jazzy was transported via ambulance to the nearest Children's hospital. She was placed into Intensive Care, barely alive. We were told by her attending physician that another day or two without treatment and she would have died. I cannot imagine the world without Jazzy in it.

The ride home from the Children's hospital was full of questions. Jazzy was an inquisitive little one. When we pulled up in front of our home, Jazzy said, "Oh my! Is this a castle? Do you have stairs in there? I have always dreamed of having stairs!" The next two years were challenging for her and us. During the first year of treatment, there were more days at the hospital than there were at home. Every time Jazzy was admitted to the hospital, me or Chuck stayed in the hospital with her. Chuck and I both maintained full-time jobs and, thankfully, were able to take vacation days, leaves of absence, and work remotely when possible. Jazzy kept a good spirit no matter how ill she was, and our kids supported her. They loved her immediately upon their first introduction.

Childhood cancer is heart-wrenching. We are thankful that she went into remission, had a world-class medical team, and had tremendous family support. Our church family stepped up to help us during that time as well. Since August of 2022, Jazzy has been cancer-free! We are thankful every day. No more chemotherapy or treatments. We have a long schedule of routine checkups ahead of us still, but thank God that, in His mercy, Jazzy has been able to beat Leukemia. God is good. Jazzy's adoption was finalized on December 18, 2020—Chuck's 57th birthday.

༒

2020 had ended well with Jazzy's adoption, but sadly, my dear mother was one of the first local COVID-19 deaths. She passed away in my home on January 22, 2020. The beginning of the year was incredibly painful, as I experienced grief and loss as never before. I knew that God would bring me comfort, just as He had through all my years of infertility, grief, and loss. God would heal, guide, and lead us.

> *Blessed are they that mourn: for they shall be comforted.*
> *— Matthew 5:4*

God is my comfort. If ever I was assured of anyone's salvation, it was my precious Mother's. I am grateful for the hope of being reunited with her again one day.

☙

In early June of 2020, Jazzy was doing so much better. Things with her were looking up. We had just endured our first Mother's Day without my own mother, and we were trying to find our new normal. I was trying to keep myself busy with work through the first year without Mom. We had received several phone calls for placement from the Department of Child Services over the past year but had declined them, as we weren't sure we would foster again. Nevertheless, one day, after hearing the story of a certain baby girl, we agreed to accept placement one more time. The plan was to go to the Neonatal Intensive Care Unit to see the baby and bond with her, then bring her home in 1-2 months when she would be healthy enough to do so. At that time, reunification with her mother and siblings was still the goal as soon as it was possible.

Mia was born at twenty-six weeks' gestation, at home, in a bathtub, during a drug binge. Mia was not taken to the hospital until five or six hours old. She was not taken by ambulance but an Uber. The driver actually carried her, hypoxic and non-responsive, into the emergency room of our local hospital. She appeared to be dead on arrival. Mia had to be resuscitated and was placed on comfort measures, as it was apparent this baby was not likely to survive the night—if she even survived transport to the nearest children's hospital more than an hour away. Still, Mia proved to be a fighter! An indestructible will to live was evident. She remained in the hospital for more than two months. She was on oxygen, a feeding tube, had a hole in her heart, and suffered periods of apnea. She was tiny but mighty. Day by day, she improved. We brought her home on July 9, 2020. We were all taken by her big, beautiful eyes and her spunk.

As is our custom, we began praying over the baby for healing and for reunification if possible. We prayed for complete restoration from circumstances that, through no fault of her own, could cause her to have lifelong issues and disability. God, in His faithfulness, restored the child to complete wellness by the end of the first year of life. She was perfect in every way and beautiful beyond words. She is a precious, curious, sassy little jewel of a human. Long black eyelashes, dark, deep, thoughtful eyes, and the ability to corral all her older siblings into doing whatever her heart desires.

Over time, it was clear this baby could not safely return to her family of origin. To further complicate things, there were more. She had four older siblings, three in the care of foster homes.

The three siblings in foster care were in two different homes. The two boys, eighteen months apart, had been in their second foster home since removal in less than six months. The sister was in her second foster home away from the boys due to behavioral issues. The three older siblings had bi-weekly visits with their mother, and the baby had been having virtual visits due to COVID-19 and illness. The siblings knew about Mia, and they had seen photos of her, but they had not met her in person.

In January of 2021, Mia's biological mother was making some strides toward reunification. Mia would return home first, and if the mother could prove her ability to care for the child, then the other siblings in foster care would follow suit. The boys needed a new placement at that time because their foster home was having trouble. Rather than send them back to the state, we insisted that they come stay with us. We would let them get to know baby Mia in our home and integrate the family prior to reunification.

On January 6, 2021, Christopher and Ian entered our home and our hearts. Christopher was three, Ian just twenty-two months. That was the first day they had met their baby sister, now nine months old.

Christopher was introverted and sweet but very much protective over anything he deemed as his. It could have been a toy he had played with at some point in the day or a chair he had sat in, even something he had placed under his blankets for safekeeping.

Then there was Ian. He was a force of independence and willfulness that I had never encountered before. The first three months, every night without fail, at bedtime, he wailed! It would last 1-3 hours every single night.

Ian also showed the same behavior in every car ride. No matter where we were going, long or short distance, he would scream in the van. Nevertheless, like with many of the other children, time has its way of sorting things out. He calmed after a while and had moments of unparalleled sweetness when he wanted it.

The attempt at reunification failed after just eighteen days. I was at the grocery store when I received the call asking if Mia could return to us. Of course, we said yes.

Meanwhile, the older sister was still in foster care. Nevaeh, now four years old, was asking why she could not live with us like her siblings. We agreed as a family that we would integrate Nevaeh into our home as well. We could not take the sadness of them being separated. Over Easter Weekend 2021, Nevaeh joined her siblings and became a part of our big, busy family.

We spent another year and a half trying to reunify. However, the mother left the state with no warning and did not try to see the children for many months. Eventually, her parental rights were terminated.

Now, in our fifties, we were parenting small children who had all been in our home for more than a year and a half. They were adoptable. We loved them, and they loved us. We had made a home for them. They had established preschools, friends, church family, our family, and extended family. They were safe and thriving. We wondered if it could really be God's will for us to adopt all these children at this stage in our lives. Still, I was continually taken back to my promise to God: "I will mother everyone you put in my life for the rest of my life. I will love all who need love and mother all who need mothered."

There was no doubt in my mind that if we did not adopt this sibling group, they would be separated. My heart could not bear the thought. After much prayer and seeking the Lord, it was clear to both Chuck and me that the children were here to stay. We had a family meeting with our children, and all agreed that though it had changed the dynamic of our home, they were our family and would be welcome and loved forever.

We were challenged by others saying we were too old, our home was already full, we were out of our minds! Our answer was, and still is: "You don't know, like we know, the conversations we have had with the Lord. You don't know the promises we have made along the way and how we know this is our assignment. This is our ministry. This is our call."

☙

December 6, 2022, was our final adoption day. The four youngest had become forever and legally our children. Our home and our hearts were full. The Scripture says that children are an heritage of the Lord, and the fruit of the womb is his reward. Happy is the man who has his quiver full of them, according to Psalm 127.

I was in prayer several months ago, worshiping, talking to God when, without any forethought, I spoke these words:

"*Thank you, Lord, for counting me worthy to be barren.*"

The words caused me to stop and reflect. Words I would have never thought possible. Without my barrenness, I would have never come to know the Lord the way that I know Him. I would have never learned to trust Him the way that I trust Him. I would have never studied or searched the Scriptures had I not been on this journey. I would have never known the love of these beautiful nine children we call our own. Or the love of another, not fully adopted, but fully ours. I would not have known the beauty of letting go—to allow His will over my desires. I am truly thankful to have been barren.

> *Sing, O barren, thou that didst not bear; break forth into singing, and cry aloud, thou that didst not travail with child: for more are the children of the desolate than the children of the married wife, saith the Lord.* — Isaiah 54:1

You can contact Sharon Aikman at:
sharon.aikman@gmail.com.

For more information on our other books and resources, special discounts, bulk purchases, or hosting a live event, please visit **www.truthbook.co.**

www.ingramcontent.com/pod-product-compliance
Lightning Source LLC
LaVergne TN
LVHW041258080426
835510LV00009B/782